AF531200

African Game-Lands

A GRAPHIC ITINERARY

IN KENYA AND ALONG THE LIVINGSTONE TRAIL IN
TANGANYIKA, BELGIAN CONGO, AND ANGOLA

1929

The giant sable's horns measured 61-1/4 inches with a 12-inch circumference at the base.

African Game-Lands

A GRAPHIC ITINERARY

IN KENYA AND ALONG THE LIVINGSTONE TRAIL IN
TANGANYIKA, BELGIAN CONGO, AND ANGOLA

1929

BY

PRENTISS N. GRAY

INTRODUCTION BY ANTHONY A. DYER

A BOOK OF THE BOONE AND CROCKETT CLUB
CONTAINING THE HUNTING AND
EXPLORATION TRAVELS OF
PRENTISS N. GRAY
AS HE CROSSES KENYA, TANGANYIKA,
BELGIAN CONGO AND
ANGOLA ON HIS SAFARI TO AFRICA.

Edited by Theodore J. Holsten, Jr. and Susan C. Reneau

The Boone and Crockett Club
Old Milwaukee Depot
250 Station Drive
Missoula, Montana 59801

AFRICAN GAME-LANDS
A Graphic Itinerary in Kenya and along the Livingstone Trail in Tanganyika, Belgian Congo and Angola
1929

by Prentiss N. Gray
Introduction by Anthony A. Dyer
Edited by Theodore J. Holsten, Jr. and Susan C. Reneau

Copyright ©1995 by the Boone and Crockett Club.

All rights reserved, including the right to reproduce this book or portions thereof in any form or by any means, electronic or mechanical, including photocopying, recording, or by any information storage and retrieval system, without permission in writing from the Boone and Crockett Club.

ISBN Number: 0-940864-23-1

Library of Congress Catalog Card Number: 95-079531

Published in October 1995
First Printing

Published in the United States of America
by the
Boone and Crockett Club
Old Milwaukee Depot
250 Station Drive
Missoula, Montana 59801-2753

(406) 542-1888

This book is dedicated to Laura Sherman Gray,
wife of Prentiss N. Gray,
who shared in his great adventure.

In search of pictures of African wildlife and specimens of rare animals and birds, representatives of the Academy of Natural Sciences of Philadelphia, Pa., went on an expedition into the heart of the wild continent. Prentiss Gray, leader of the party and his wife, are shown in one of the all-steel photographic autos which were being utilized on the expedition.

Foreword

THEODORE J. HOLSTEN, JR.

Soon after Prentiss N. Gray became president of the J. Henry Schroder Banking Corporation in 1923, he helped make the New York bank's operation so successful during the difficult times that he was afforded the right to unlimited vacation time. This enabled him to make numerous trips throughout North America.

He was an avid photographer and many of his outstanding still photographs were used to illustrate the book, *From the Peace to the Fraser*, which was published by the Boone and Crockett Club in 1994 from his extensive journals of trips taken between 1900 and 1930. His travels took him to remote areas and his discovery of a new low-altitude pass through the Canadian Rockies produced a fellowship in the Royal Geographic Society in London, which published the description of "Gray Pass."

In 1929, Prentiss Gray, who was a trustee of the Philadelphia Academy of Natural Sciences, undertook an extended expedition to Africa on behalf of the Academy. A special report, issued by the Academy, includes the following:

In this most interesting account of the movements of the Gray African Expedition, Mr. Gray modestly refrains from mentioning more than incidentally the success of the Expedition in securing a large number of splendid still photographs of many species of African game as well as thousands of feet of even more valuable motion picture films. These photographs, both motion and still, form one of the most important records of wildlife in Africa ever made. With many species of these mammals becoming rarer yearly, the Academy is the fortunate possessor of a record of what has well been called the closing scenes of the "Age of Mammals." Mrs. Gray, a Life Member of the Academy, accompanied her husband in much of his East African work, and the thanks of the Academy are extended to her, as well to Mr. Gray, for the splendid results of the Expedition. Mr. W. Wedgwood Bowen, who is now a member of the scientific staff of the Academy,

FORTY FIVE WEST
FORTY FIFTH STREET
NEW YORK CITY

ELTINGE F. WARNER
PUBLISHER

Gray

OUR CONSERVATION COUNCIL

D. R. ANTHONY, JR.
Congressman; joint Introducer of the Game Refuge Bill.

HORACE M. ALBRIGHT
Superintendent of Yellowstone National Park.

BROOKE ANDERSON
Member of the Federal Advisory Board of the Migratory Bird Treaty Act.

J. B. HARKIN
Commissioner of the Canadian National Parks.

GEORGE A. LAWYER
Former Chief United States Game Warden.

WM. B. MERSHON
Sportsman — Author — Conservationist.

E. W. NELSON
Chief of the U. S. Biological Survey.

HARRY S. NEW
U. S. Postmaster General; joint Introducer of the Game Refuge Bill in the United States Senate.

T. GILBERT PEARSON
President of the National Association of Audubon Societies.

THEO. ROOSEVELT
First Executive Chairman of the National Conference on Outdoor Recreation.

August 9th, 1927

The Explorers Club,
47 West 76th Street,
New York, N. Y.

Gentlemen:-

I have known Mr. Prentis N. Gray for a number of years and can, without any hesitancy, assure you that he would be a very desirable member for the Explorers Club. Mr. Gray has made some of the finest motion pictures that I have ever seen of the white tailed deer, as well as numerous other varieties of game throughout the United States and Canada.

Personally, he is a very fine type and I feel certain that the Membership Committee would do well in choosing to make him a member of the Club.

Very truly yours,

Harold McCracken
Associate Editor.

HMC:FT

Harold McCracken, well-known author and associate editor of *Field & Stream* magazine, seconded the nomination of Prentiss N. Gray as associate member of The Explorers Club in 1927. McCracken's letter of nomination is shown here.

was responsible for the important and extensive ornithological collection secured, as well as other new or little known zoological material.

Prentiss Gray described the objectives of the expedition as follows:

When the expedition set out from Philadelphia last March, we had three objectives: to bring back to the Academy a series of motion pictures of East African game; to secure a group of giant sable antelope (Hippotragus niger variani) and to obtain a representative collection of the birds of Angola. Our ideas expanded as we progressed, and while we still held to the main objectives, we did broaden our scope to include the only motion pictures taken of the total eclipse of the sun on May ninth; a group of Hunter's antelope (Damaliscus hunteri) from the lower Tana River in Kenya; a group of Waller's gazelle or gerenuk (Lithocranius walleri) from Northern Kenya; and about six hundred birds from Kenya and Tanganyika.

One of the sad aftermaths of Gray's many trips and expeditions is the total deterioration of his extensive motion picture films. As happened with so many early films produced by Hollywood, chemical deterioration with age reduced them to dust.

The giant sable or "royal sable" as described in Rowland Ward's *Records of Big Game* occupied a limited area in Angola between the Upper Cuanza River and its tributary, the Luando, on a wooded tableland about 3,700 feet high. No new specimens have been recorded since the 1950s and with a lack of conservation efforts resulting from the continuous civil war in Angola over many recent years, the species is probably now extinct. The giant sable taken by Prentiss Gray for the Academy of Natural Sciences has a horn length of 61-1/4 inches. The World's Record giant sable has 64-7/8 inch horns.

I had the opportunity to visit the Academy of Natural Sciences in Philadelphia recently where I saw the diorama of the giant sable secured by Prentiss Gray. It is interesting that Gray's 1929 expedition was unable to secure a complete family group of giant sable. The weather and season turned against him and he had to leave Angola without completing this objective. Gray subsequently sponsored the Gray Second African Expedition of 1930, which was led by Harold T. Green, curator of museum exhibits for the Academy. Gray did not personally participate in the

A Grant's gazelle in Northern Kenya

Second Expedition. This expedition achieved the desired results and also enabled W.W. Bowen to more extensively complete his ornithological studies and collection.

An interesting aspect of the Academy of Natural Sciences is the heavy involvement of several Boone and Crockett Club members. Prentiss Gray and his friend, R.R.M. Carpenter, donated the antelope diorama from specimens secured in Wyoming on behalf of the Academy in 1934. Carpenter, along with his son, William K. Carpenter, and Harry Whitney were all trustees of the Academy as well as Boone and Crockett Club members. This group of prominent sportsmen donated a great many of the Academy's impressive dioramas of big game of the world.

In 1927, Prentiss Gray was elected to associate membership in The Explorers Club. His sponsor, William M. Newsom, wrote, "I might mention he has the finest still and motion pictures of deer I have ever seen and at present is working on a series of motion pictures of horned game of North America of which deer, elk and antelope are completed."

Gray's nomination was seconded by Harold McCracken, well-known author and associate editor of *Field & Stream* magazine. His nomination was also seconded by James L. Clark. In 1931, Gray applied for and was elected to full active membership in the prestigious organization. His sponsor was William J. Morden who, along with James L. Clark, was one of the best-known names associated with the American Museum of Natural History. Clark was a regular member of the Boone and Crockett Club.

Prentiss Gray was killed in 1935 in a tragic boating accident while enroute to join his friend, R.R.M. Carpenter, for a hunting trip in the Florida Everglades. He packed a lot of adventure and accomplishment into his short, fifty-year life.

Theodore J. Holsten, Jr., is chairman of the Boone and Crockett Club's Editorial and Publications Committee and editor of this book and *From the Peace to the Fraser* (1994). He has been a member of the Club since 1986. Holsten is a columnist for the Club's national magazine, *Fair Chase, The Official Publication of the Boone and Crockett Club.* Holsten collects and deals in rare books of hunting, guns, adventure, exploration, natural history and fishing.

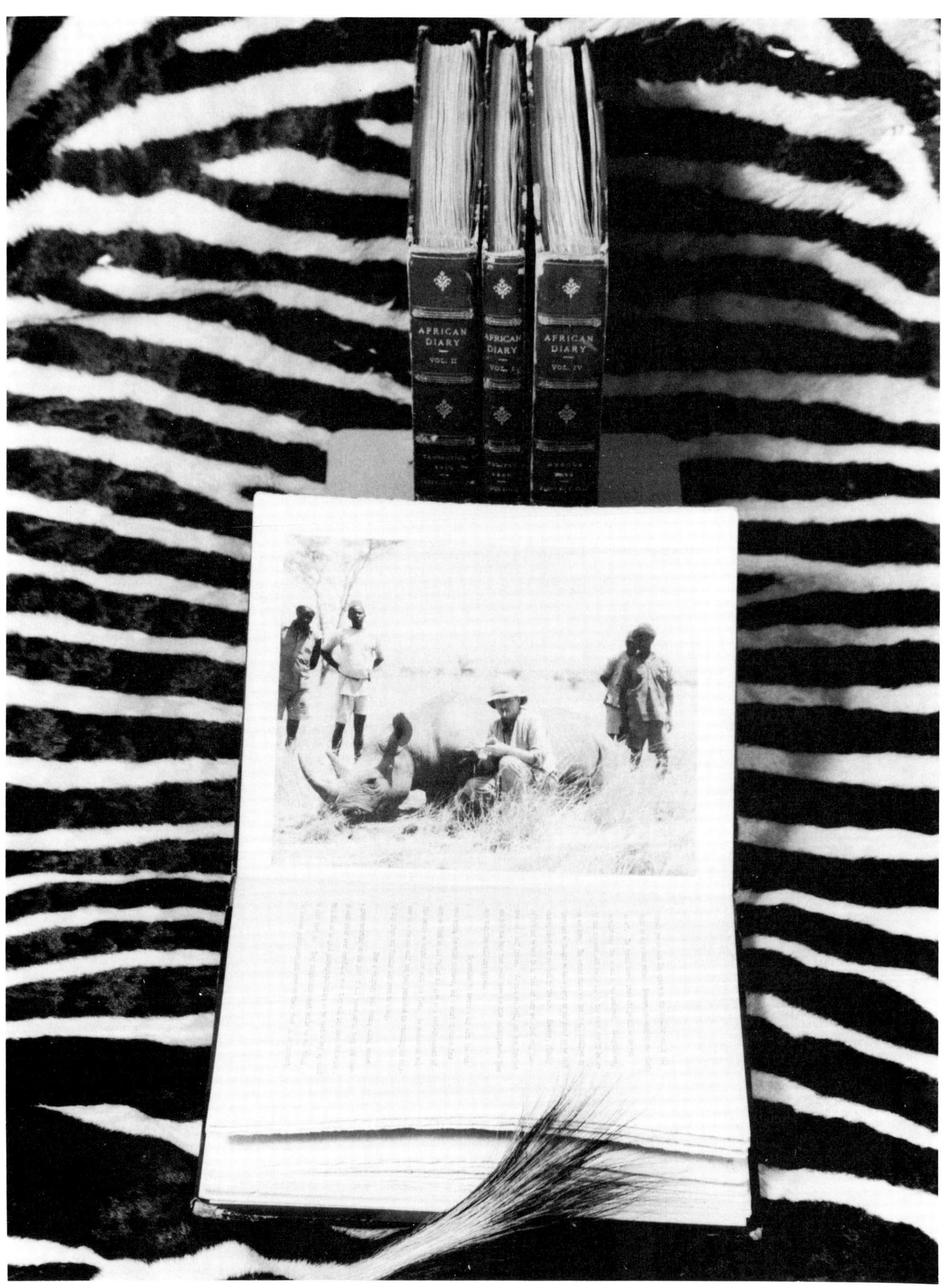

Four original, leather-bound journals of Prentiss N. Gray, written in 1929, became the basis for the new Boone and Crockett Club book, *African Game-Lands.* The journals are shown against a zebra pelt belonging to Philip L. and Hedwig Wright of Missoula, Montana, who went on African safari in 1991.

Prologue

SUSAN C. RENEAU

Prentiss N. Gray's fascination with wildlife began as a young man growing up and hunting in Northern California. In the book, *From the Peace to the Fraser*, Prentiss tells of his blacktail deer hunt in Humboldt County, California, and of his efforts to introduce deer to the Golden Gate Park in San Francisco. This same young man assisted residents of San Francisco after the earthquake of 1906 as captain of the University of California-Berkeley militia and organized the Commission for Relief in Belgium during World War I after being appointed to do the job by Herbert Hoover.

Prentiss began at age 18 in 1900 to record his thoughts and experiences. This writing process eventually led to a series of twenty-one typed and leather-bound journals that spanned his adult life from 1900 to 1935. Inspiration for Prentiss' journals were his two sisters, Mabel and Elizabeth, who were not allowed to go on his many outdoor adventures, but insisted he write a diary of each trip to share with them. His son, Sherman, said that every night on every trip for the rest of his life, no matter what the weather or his physical condition, his father wrote in his diary, and at the conclusion of each trip, "packed off" a well-illustrated account of what had happened to his sisters and to the rest of the family.

Unique to Prentiss Gray's travels were his efforts to include his wife, Laura Sherman Gray, on many of these adventurous hunting and exploration treks, including the lengthy African safari. Prentiss married Laura in 1908 and found her an able companion. Her impressions of their travels are included in the journals along with Prentiss Gray's observations. Adventure of this young couple began on their honeymoon when they traveled to the west coast of Central America and visited the newly constructed Panama Canal in May of 1908. During one of their North American trips, guides for the couple saw Laura as the Greek goddess, "Diana."

Each passing year, Prentiss went on more ambitious trips and grew more preoccupied with photography. On each hunting expedition, the difficulty and excitement of capturing wildlife on film became more important to him than the normal hunt with a rifle, Sherman said. His trips became more lengthy as he achieved greater success in the banking industry.

"The pattern of his hunting diaries bears this out when one sees that he at first went for relatively short trips to eastern Canada, then, as the years passed, his trips got longer and more elaborate in the western United States and Canada, culminating in a full year's safari in Africa," Sherman said.

Prentiss Gray's photographic and written record of wildlife throughout the world became a permanent record of 20th century explorers to glorify the environment and nature's wonders. Gray's enthusiasm to record his discoveries become the backdrop for *African Game-Lands.*

The editors of *The Sportsman* magazine in 1930 asked Gray to write a series of articles about his African safari. Their brief introduction reads:

African big-game shooting is no novelty either to the American sportsman or to the American public. The rotogravure sections of our daily papers have published many fine pictures taken by the Carl Akeleys, the Martin Johnsons, the George Eastmans, and others. Books have been written on shooting in Africa, in all its phases. Movies have been shown of water holes and prairie herds. Vast numbers of heads of African game look down on their collectors from library walls or dens or banquet halls.

In publishing the accompanying manuscript and photographs we are conscious that we are not adding a series of new discoveries to the existing store of sporting or scientific knowledge concerning African wild life [sic]. We do feel, however, that this presents a splendid example of the right approach toward big-game shooting, and of the rich rewards which await the right-minded sportsman in Africa.

Mr. Prentiss N. Gray made the long trip to Africa, East and West, primarily for the joy of adventuring afield, of seeing new lands and new species of wild animals. He finds no pleasure in unnecessary slaughter. Rather he prefers to retain a tangible record of the wild living beauty which he found there. The illustrations in (these articles) are eloquent witnesses to his distinction as an amateur photographer. The whole record is that of a gentleman sportsman.

Gray is best known to the hunting world as the first editor and designer of the

Boone and Crockett Club's famous book, *Records of North American Big Game*, which was first published in 1932. With the death of Gray, the second edition of *Records of North American Big Game* was delayed until 1939.

Our deep understanding of Prentiss Gray has come, once again, because of his only son, Sherman, who shared one of his most prized possessions with readers by loaning his father's travel and adventure journals to the Boone and Crockett Club. Sherman Gray's detailed biography of his father in *From the Peace to the Fraser* traces Gray's life from his birth in 1884 to his untimely and tragic death in 1935 and offers more fascinating facts about this unique 20th century conservationist. Sherman was only 16 years old when his beloved father died. He writes:

"I remember the event as an abrupt shattering of an idyllic sojourn at boarding school. Things were much more serious after that and the process of growing up was greatly accelerated. The times that I treasured the most with my father were those which even now appeal to a 16-year-old boy; a pack trip across the Thorofare Plateau in Wyoming; a moose hunt on the Cascapedia River in Quebec; and, an extended hunting trip in Alaska. It took me a long time to realize that, by age 16, without revealing his motives, Prent Gray had furnished me with the qualifications (three North American big-game trophies) to join his favorite group, the Boone and Crockett Club. I was very proud to be able to do this 32 years later."

Prentiss Gray never lived to see Sherman Gray grow to adulthood. Turn back the pages of time to 1929 and explore the vastness of early 20th century Africa as you come with Prentiss and Laura Gray on their trip of a lifetime to Africa in *African Game-Lands.*

Susan C. Reneau is co-editor of this book as well as *Records of North American Big Game, 10th Edition (1993); From the Peace to the Fraser (1994); Records of North American Whitetail Deer, 3rd Edition (1995), Boone and Crockett Club's 22nd Big Game Awards, 1992 1994* (1995). She is co-author of the book, *Colorado's Biggest Bucks and Bulls* (1983, 1984, 1988, 1990) and author of *The Adventures of Moccasin Joe: True Life Story of Sgt. George S. Howard, 1872 to 1877 (1994).* Susan holds a M.S. in Business Marketing and Public Relations from American University and a B.A. in Education and Speech Communication from the University of Northern Colorado.

A map drawn by Prentiss N. Gray shows the route he took on his trip through central Africa. Gray's trip crossed Kenya, Tanganyika, Belgian Congo and Angola in 1929. Specimens of big game, birds and fish from this expedition became a part of the permanent collections of The Academy of Natural Sciences of Philadelphia.

Introduction

Anthony A. Dyer

These personal journals tell of a safari that took place sixty-six years ago. The journals were written to be read by the author's sisters and, therefore, a lot remains unsaid because he did not need to give them details they already knew.

By today's standards, you may be surprised in the way some of the hunting took place. In those far-off days, lion were abundant in Africa and were considered vermin. The codes of conduct for the sporting hunting of African big game were yet to be established. People shot animals indiscriminately from trains, river boats and whatever motorized vehicles they could ride to within shooting range.

At that time, visiting sportsmen put too much faith in the underpowered Springfield .30-06 and Winchester .30-30 that had served them so well in their homelands. Some of those rifles were inaccurate by today's standards. Now we try our best to achieve clean, one-shot kills. So much trouble and disaster has been caused by the casual pulling of a trigger on the first shot.

In defense of some of the poor shooting told of in this book, it must be said that the telescopic sights that allow us such precision today generally were not available. The use of scopes was considered by most people to be unsporting and there still remain some people who are prepared to risk the wounding of animals because of their own view of what is sport hunting. There is a fine line dividing the two sides of this argument, but in a world where hunters are the targets for ever-increasing opposition, we must refine our hunting practices to the highest possible standards.

Over the years, hunting methods in East Africa have changed. In 1929, people could and did shoot lion regardless of licenses. Later, game licenses specified a limit of four lion each year. Not until 1959 did I succeed in persuading the Uganda Game Department to remove lion from the vermin list! Today a hunter needs a special and relatively expensive license to shoot one lion.

There were other differences between the safaris of then and now. The whole pace of life was different. Prentiss Gray took a year off to enjoy his safari. Had he planned to do the same trip today he would have allowed a maximum of three months.

My life spans these changes and I knew some of the people Prentiss Gray hunted with in Kenya in what was then called Tanganyika. I am also fortunate to have hunted with Americans of his generation. This was a generation of people who held fast and true to the old values. These were men amongst men, proud patriots and warriors, great hunters and sportsmen.

Prentiss Gray managed relief work with great distinction in Belgium in World War I. Two of my safari clients joined Kermit Roosevelt's Independent American Brigade and fought in France before the United States of America joined the war. One was Col. Dean Witter, who founded the bank of that name, and the other was Charles Renaud, who later became one of the most highly respected oil geologists in the American oil business. A third friend of similar stature was Charles Crisp, who, while serving with the Marines in China, took leave and mounted an expedition to be probably the last American to hunt the great sheep in those remote mountains. Having known and greatly admired these three men, I feel I know the kind of man that Prentiss Gray was.

The editors of this book have asked me to tell you about Philip Percival, who conducted Prentiss Gray's safari. I first met the Percival family in 1938 and have remained friends with the descendants of that fine family for the last fifty-seven years. Philip Percival was the first president of the East African Professional Hunters' Association for the first sixteen years of its life, and I held that position for the last thirteen years, until we disbanded in 1977. I am the custodian of its records and the survivors still have reunions to try to ensure the ethics and traditions that have come to us from people like Prentiss Gray and Philip Percival should not be lost.

The minutes of the committee meetings of the East African Professional Hunters' Association have repeated references showing Philip Percival's concern for all matters to do with conservation and sport hunting. A group of professional hunters were the founding body of most of the national parks of East Africa. In his annual report for 1951, Philip Percival expressed his concern that a modern car of the Jeep type had pushed into the country where once the game was unmolested. In my own history of those days I added that the advent of the four-wheel drive vehicle was the death knell of the proper hunting safari, for it had become too easy for any good bush driver to go bouncing around the country, covering miles and achieving a bag that had previously only been obtained by hard and skillful hunting. I had at that time already covered 60,000 miles of Africa before I was introduced to the luxurious ease of four-wheel drive.

Philip Percival was considered the dean of hunters and was the idol of us youngsters. He was our authority on how to hunt a wounded lion or Cape buffalo, or what was the best gun, or how to treat a difficult client. He was our leader, spokesman and example in all things. We were, I suppose, immensely proud of him because there existed a chance for each of us to do as he had done. If we, in our own estimation, did so, then we had reached the pinnacle.

He came to British East Africa, as Kenya was then called, in 1905 and within five days already had been indoctrinated into the noble sport of lion hunting on horseback. Soon he had seen two friends mauled, one of whom died. For the rest of his active years, he had a passion for fast riding over rough ground. His own words will give you a description of what rough ground means:

"To give you an idea of how bad the going was on that particular vlei (dried up grassy water pan), we had five out of eight horses down on one chase during the Roosevelt safari."

His safari career spanned fifty years and he had many memorable safari clients and pays this tribute to one of them.

"The Roosevelt safari still holds its own as a great and memorable experience. I then met and came to know a famous man who added up to everything I had previously heard about him."

The Boone and Crockett Club has led the way in promoting and guarding the management of wildlife and maintaining the highest standards in hunting and conservation. Theodore Roosevelt founded this club in 1887 and more than 100 years later it is evident it is more important than ever before that we should all fight for world-wide acceptance of the Boone and Crockett Club's principals of Fair Chase.

Unlike Prentiss Gray, Philip Percival enjoyed a long life. As with Prentiss Gray, Percival enjoyed an exciting life, too. Percival was on active service in both world wars and in 1961 he killed two stock-raiding lions with a right and left from his old .450 No. 2, on his seventy-sixth birthday.

Reading this book you will come to the conclusion that Prentiss Gray was an able and determined sportsman. The only real and repeated complaints he made were that he suffered from the cold in Equatorial Africa. He worked long and hard, and with great patience, to take excellent photographs. In those days the equipment was awkward and bulky. He was frequently up half the night loading films for the next day. In this pioneer work he was some years ahead of the famous Martin Johnson expeditions.

Collecting museum specimens is a specialized business. The field preparations of the skin for a full body mount is not easy. When Prentiss Gray left Philip Percival's team behind him, he collected and prepared giant sable specimens in Angola. He hunted, shot and skinned these magnificent animals virtually by himself. The description of that hunt is an epic tale in itself.

There is refreshing honesty and modesty in Prentiss Gray's accounts that make them important descriptions of an era that is gone in the same way as the great clipper ships have vanished from the sea. We are fortunate to have this book as a permanent record of a short and unique period of hunting history.

Anthony A. Dyer lives on Kisima Farm near Nairobi, Kenya. During his long career as a professional hunter, he was associated with Philip Percival who conducted the East African portion of the Gray African Safari. Dyer was the last president of the East African Professional Hunters' Association that was disbanded in 1977. His much sought after limited edition book, *The East African Hunters*, chronicles the history of that organization that did much to promote conservation and hunting ethics.

Acknowledgements

Janet E. Baldwin, curator of collections for The Explorers Club, New York City, who provided information on Prentiss N. Gray's membership in that organization.

Joe Coogan, feature editor for *Petersen's HUNTING* magazine, who lived in Africa and offered his knowledge of the continent by identifying unique terminology and geographic locations not found in normal reference books.

Glen Cottar, professional hunter in Nairobi, who assisted in our contacts with Anthony A. Dyer.

Elaine Cummings, an editor for Safari Club International, who provided assistance during the editing process of *African Game-Lands* by identifying the proper spellings of big game.

Sherman Gray, son of Prentiss N. Gray, who loaned his father's original, leather-bound exploration journals of Africa to the Boone and Crockett Club to produce *African Game-Lands.*

Carol Kersavage, editor of Outdoor Writers Association of America, who reviewed the African journals and copy edited the book manuscript.

Jack Reneau, director of big game records for the Boone and Crockett Club, who provided continued assistance and identification of geographic locations.

Halcyon albiventris prentissgrayi was named for Prentiss N. Gray.

ACKNOWLEDGEMENTS

Carol M. Spawn, manuscript/librarian for the Philadelphia Academy of Natural Sciences, who researched background information on Prentiss N. Gray's activities with the Academy as a trustee and expedition sponsor.

Harry Tennison, for his assistance in contacting Tony Dyer and in editing the glossary of African words and expressions.

Julie L. Tripp, art director for the Boone and Crockett Club, who offered her graphic design expertise in all phases of production and marketing and scanned all Prentiss N. Gray photographs that appear in this book.

Duane Walker, whose wonderful artistic talent went into the design of the *African Game-Lands* dust jacket.

Ludo J. Wurfbain of Safari Press who loaned reference books and a glossary of terms to clarify the spellings of African geographic terminology and wild animals.

Prentiss N. Gray carries his state-of-the-art camera equipment to photograph wildlife.

Books by Prentiss N. Gray:

Records of North American Big Game - 1932 (Editor)

Hunting Trails on Three Continents - 1933 (Co-Editor)

From the Peace to the Fraser: Newly Discovered North American Hunting and Exploration Journals, 1900 to 1930 - 1994 (Author, Posthumously)

African Game-Lands: A Graphic Itinerary in Kenya and along the Livingstone Trail in Tanganyika, Belgian Congo and Angola, 1929 - 1995 (Author, Posthumously)

Contents

"There was not a maned head in the bunch so we devoted all our thoughts to photographs."

Illustrations

ILLUSTRATIONS

African Game-Lands

A GRAPHIC ITINERARY

IN KENYA AND ALONG THE LIVINGSTONE TRAIL IN TANGANYIKA, BELGIAN CONGO, AND ANGOLA

1929

Dr. Harlan Stetson, left, and Prentiss N. Gray, right, stand beside the multiple chronograph as they prepare to study the total eclipse in 1929. Stetson was a member of the Harvard University Eclipse Expedition who asked Prentiss and Laura to join the scientific party.

ECLIPSE

PART ONE

MISSING A TIGER AND SHOOTING THE SUN

WHERE can we begin this trip? Certainly not at New York, where the only thing novel about our departure was the day, March 13, 1929, and everything else all the way to San Francisco was as usual. Travel ceases to be an event when you can call all the telegraph poles along the railroad right-of-way by their first names; not even at San Francisco when the ship pulled away from the dock with the band playing and all the family enthusiastically waving handkerchiefs to speed us on our way straight into the lion's maw or the soft embrace of a tsetse fly. The Golden Gate was old stuff - always beautiful but not new enough after many passages through it when I was young - to mark the starting point of this trip to Africa of which I had dreamed for twenty years and actively planned for six years.

After all, I presume an African trip cannot start until you get to Africa and as we were going the long way around the world to get to the promised land, and much did happen enroute, we possibly should call San Francisco the start of the trip that started the trip to Africa.

There the "S.S. President Wilson" cast off her lines on March 22nd and we watched the Ferry Building and Telegraph Hill disappear in the haze. The wreck of the steamer "Coos Bay" on Mile Rock skippered by my old friend, Bror Olsen, wakened our sympathies but soon we were over the Potato Patch and the long roll of the Pacific began to take toll of our fellow passengers.

Honolulu six days later, on March 29th, was something of a blue haze. Possibly it was the bootleg liquor provided by McCoy, an old friend of Food Administration

Kyoto was full of temples. Prent wanted to visit the municipal baths.

days, or possibly it was the unusual heat (They use the word unusual just as freely in Honolulu as in Southern California, and of course we landed there on an unusually hot day.) At any rate it was darn hot and, despite a swim at Waikiki, we were glad to get back to the "Wilson" for the late afternoon sailing.

We settled down there for the first long leg of the journey, thirteen days, although a tournament of deck sports, a fancy dress ball, a real Easter parade wherein a few fools (myself included) took most of the prizes for displaying what the well-dressed women on Fifth Avenue were wearing, made it seem more like thirteen hours, so quickly did the time fly by.

About in the middle of this I had a fit of what Laura calls planning. I began to pore over maps and ask impertinent questions of the crew and passengers. I fell off my feed and displayed all the evidence of getting ready for a new hunting trip. Out

Laura spent her time in the shops of Shanghai.

Straggling up the hills lay Hong Kong.

"We docked at Kowloon and crossed on the ferry to Hong Kong."

of it came this cerebration. Tigers lay in waiting along our course. They were most frequently met with in Johore. The Sultan of Johore had a large harem. The younger officers of the bank back in New York ought to have some influence with the ladies of this harem to persuade the Sultan to lead forth a tiger and put salt on his tail so I could hit him with the .465 Holland. So I sent frantic cables to the bank and received the following reply:

Received from Baron Schroder:[1]
Said the wicked old King of Johore
Of women I've many a score
But I can't oblige Prent
If his fancy is bent
On a tiger instead of a - _______

I was forced to reply by cable at once:
Tell the Baron's old friend of Johore
That the lady in question's a bore.
I'm of much finer fibre
I want but a tiger
Let Bruno run up his own score.

After this I got action, whether through the harem or not I don't know, and soon Singapore wired me that the Sultan had given in, and the tiger hunt was on.

While I was interviewing all the passengers on the boat about shooting tiger, I found we had on board an expedition sent by Harvard University to do a little shooting in tigerland, only they were after the whole works, the sun, moon and stars, and figured to line up the first two so they could get them with one pot shot. Game hogs, I call them, to come all around the world and then sit and wait till the moon and sun were exactly in line from a point called Alor Star in Kedah. Then, for 299 seconds, they proposed to shoot all the film they had out of sundry cameras. Not content with all the equipment they had brought along, they enlisted my eleven

[1] In 1929, Prentiss Gray was president of J. Henry Schroder Banking Corporation of New York, a wholly owned subsidiary of J. Henry Schroder & Co. of London whose chairman was Baron Bruno Schroder.

Vendors in a Hong Kong market peer at passing visitors.

cameras and made me agree to go with them on this pot-shooting solar eclipse expedition.

On April 11th we came to Kobe and luck was with us, for the cherry blossoms were at their height and the countryside was all ablaze. As we did not get ashore until afternoon, we confined ourselves to riding around Kobe in jinrikishas and dining at Kikusui where, in true Japanese style, they took your shoes away as soon as you crossed the threshold. A couple of good-looking dolls ushered us into a paper-walled room and motioned us to squat on the floor around a little table twelve inches high. We sat there until our knees ached while the two damsels cooked up a mess of beef and vegetables over two charcoal braziers that they put in the center of the table. Then they gave us each a raw egg and a bowl of rice. We broke the egg into a small dish and stirred it vigorously while the cooking went on. At last they announced in good Japanese that "diner est servi" and left us. We had no idea what to do with it, and there was no window out of which to pour it. Finally, we scooped the Irish stew out of the cooking pans, poured in our scrambled eggs and, when thoroughly cooked, put them in the stew. Then we threw all manners to the winds, for we were famished, and fairly shoveled our rice, eggs and stew into our mouths with the chopsticks. When we reached the boat, the steward showed us how daintily you could transfer a foot of string beef, two carrots and a leek on two chopsticks from the cooking pot to the stirred egg dish. There they cooled and were then removed to the rice bowl where you added a half pound of rice and got it all into your mouth without dropping so much as a grain of rice on the teak table. As we sailed before dinner the next day, I never had a chance to try it.

We slept ashore that night and the next day left early for Kyoto. I don't know why we chose Kyoto except it was only two hours away and was full of temples. There are 1,109 of them and I'll bet I was dragged to every one. Roger Sherman[2] and I tried twice to escape and visit the municipal baths where we were told the bathing was not only "mixed" but "au naturel." We were captured and hauled back to the temples both times. As temples they were not much, but as a background for blossoming cherry trees they were a riot. The impression I always want to keep of Kyoto is splashes of dainty pink sprays among the evergreens.

We sailed at dark and had a wonderful view of the twinkling lights of Kobe as we passed along the front.

I have always wanted to see Shanghai. I lost a lot of money once in a business

"We feasted our eyes on the magnificent panorama of deep blue bay with its lazy junks."

in Shanghai and I guess my curiosity was a desire to see how big a rat hole it was to swallow up so much in a short time. We landed at the customs landing on the Bund and were met by the Hagers,[3] who took us at once to their house. This was a relief, both from the ship and from the usual hotels ashore, as I was recovering from my second typhoid inoculation and felt like a boiled owl. It was a godsend.

There is not much to say about Shanghai. Laura spent her time in the shops and acquired a lot of junk, and I walked about the streets marveling at the lack of brains that prompted a style of architecture that was a poor copy of Paris, Brussels or London and as unsuited to China as it could possibly be. Nowhere in the city did I see one building that showed any attempt to take a Chinese motif and adapt it to modern necessities.

The country clubs were splendid and outdid in equipment many around New York, but the buildings, while well-built and expensive, would have been more suitable in Hoboken. This attitude of the foreign residents to get as far away as possible from anything Chinese is possibly understandable. The native city is indescribably filthy and we did not penetrate far into it as an epidemic of smallpox and spinal meningitis was raging. We smelled all of it we cared to.

The following morning at 6 a.m. (The skipper had a mania for arriving and departing at 6 a.m.) we sailed, but about 10 a.m. close to the mouth of the river we stuck fast in the mud. For two hours we churned away in twenty-five feet of water and six feet of soft mud while the ship was drawing thirty-one feet. It looked for a time as if we would not get over the bar of the Yangtze but persistence and a rising tide made it possible and we were off to Hong Kong.

Once more we had a chance to say "came the dawn," for the first officer called us at 4 a.m. so we could see the entrance to the harbor. It was a truly wonderful sight as we steamed in through the narrow passages until, just as it was getting light, we entered Lyee-mun Pass, which is only three-eighths of a mile wide. Beyond, straggling up the hills, lay Hong Kong on the island and Kowloon opposite on the mainland. We docked at Kowloon and crossed on the ferry to Hong Kong, where

[2] Roger Sherman was the younger brother of Prentiss' wife, Laura. Roger and his wife, Claudine, accompanied the Gray's on the "S.S. President Wilson" to Japan and then returned home to California.

[3] Reed Hager, a son of the Hager family in Shanghai, was a vice president of the Schroder Bank in New York.

Little lizards that gallop over the ceiling of a room were considered absolutely necessary for a well-furnished house.

the endless shopping for souvenirs by the women started all over again. I dragged them away at 11 a.m. for a motor trip around the island. We climbed a magnificent road to the top of the ridge and dropped down a long grade to Repulse Bay where there is a splendid hotel on a beach better than Waikiki. We rested for a couple of hours with occasional "Singapore Slings" interspersed, and feasted our eyes on the magnificent panorama of deep blue bay with its lazy junks while above towered the rugged mountains.

The British have done magnificent work in building roads on the island. All drainage from the hillsides, which apparently at times is torrential, is led off in concrete gutters and conducted under the roads in masonry culverts. Just at the moment there was a drought of rather a serious nature so the hillsides looked dry and parched, but when it rains there must be a lot of water coming down suddenly judging from the size of the drains.

The rest of our visit was given up to strolling through the native city, which is infinitely cleaner than Shanghai. Toward evening we returned to the ship and threw pennies overboard for which the Chinese kids dived. The water of the harbor was so clean I wanted to go in myself but some of the people on the junks, that swarmed around the ship day and night, had evidently never fallen overboard. On the morning of April 21st we sailed, and from the flying bridge of the ship I took pictures of the harbor as we steamed out.

Long before daylight on April 23rd the captain called us to see Corregidor (Philippines) and he chose the same unearthly hour of 6 a.m. to steam in through the breakwater of Manila Harbor. About 9 a.m., after we had passed all sorts of passport and medical examinations, James Ross and Ewald Selph of the law firm of Ross, Lawrence and Selph came aboard and took us in charge. From that moment onward we never saw an idle moment. Lunch at the Army and Navy Club, tea at the Manila Club, dinner at the Polo Club, auto rides to Pasig. There was no end to it. We came ashore to the Manila Hotel for a change and were greatly amused by the little lizards that gallop over the ceiling of the room. They are considered absolutely necessary adjuncts to any well-furnished house.

An old high school friend whom I had not seen for twenty-eight years, Whipple Hall and his wife, who was Ethel Crellin, hunted us up and we had tea at their lovely home. We fairly staggered aboard ship at the end of the second day loaded with hats and embroidered dresses and full of food.

The rest house at Batu Pahat was a clean and proper place.

"We built palm shelters for the cameras and apparatus to observe the eclipse."

It is a 1,300 mile pull from Manila to Singapore and for four lazy days we sailed over tropical seas. It was very hot and not a breath of air so we just sat. We came to feel like the two old fellows on a hot day in Arkansas who were sitting on the porch with their feet cocked up against a post.

One said, "Bill, here comes Judge Powers' funeral down the street."

Bill replied, "I sure wish I was facing t'other way so I could see it."

Once more at 6 a.m. the skipper made a port. This does not sound very early but it really means getting up at 4:30 or 5 a.m. to see us come in - standing around for the doctor till 7 a.m., grabbing some breakfast and dashing ashore to run all over the town till the small hours of the next morning. This time it was Singapore on May 29th and as this was the start of my tiger hunt, we were all agog.

Harry Gild, who had arranged the shoot, met us at the dock and after dropping Laura at the Europe Hotel and persuading her to buy a wagon load of silver dishes that were said to be sold to save a minor sultan from the bankruptcy court, he raced me all over town buying helmets, khaki clothes, white suits, etc.

We were away in a motor the next day at 7 a.m., and with every turn of the wheel Gild told us how this particular tiger they had rounded up in the jungle was crying out loud for one of my .465 bullets. In between times he expostulated on how lucky we were to have asked him to fix it because no one else could have persuaded the Sultan to let us shoot this kind-faced pet cat of his.

In the middle of one of these orations, we went around a curve at forty-five miles an hour and, bang, went a tire. In an instant we stuck our radiator into the bank, slid the rear end completely around as the other three tires blew and slammed up against the rock wall. It was over before we could think and we pinched ourselves to see if we were alive. We were, and unhurt, but the car was a mess. We started repairs and after about an hour a friend of Gild's, Mr. Marshall, director of mines for Johore, showed up and took Laura and me on to Batu Pahat. Gild afterwards caught another car and followed us with the luggage.

At Batu Pahat we were taken to the rest house maintained by the government. This was the pleasantest kind of surprise for I had a vague notion we had to sleep in the jungle but here was a clean, proper place with delicious food.

We had a bite of lunch and then drove ten miles farther. Here we found about thirty men by the side of the road by a path leading off into the jungle. I was led along this path for a mile to a small clearing where the jungle had been cut back a

The cherry blossoms in Kyoto were at their height and the countryside was all ablaze in Japan.

"The water of the harbor was so clean I wanted to go in myself but some of the people on the junks . . . had evidently never fallen overboard."

few feet. I was stationed in this clearing with the solid wall of jungle tangle more than forty feet away. After a wait of fifteen minutes Captain Ahmed blew a trumpet and a roar arose in a half circle in front of us about half a mile away. Such a din of horns, firecrackers and beating on the tin pans as I never heard. It sounded like Chinese New Year.

For three quarters of an hour this kept up. Sometimes the ki-yi-ing of small dogs started them off again if it had died down a little. It was a terrible din coming out of the dark jungle, and on top of all this I was informed that the tiger was supposed to pop out not more than forty feet away. I'll tell the world I was not having a good time. However, I looked behind me and spied another official, Shat Datok, leaning nonchalantly on his malacca stick smoking a cigar. No gun, no sword - he was paying my marksmanship too large a compliment. To add to the rest of my anxiety, I knew I had to shoot straight or we would have a dead Datok on our hands if that tiger got to us.

It seemed a week before I saw the brush move and after being sure it was not the tiger, made out a beater. The drive was over and the trumpet call brought them all out of the bush. There were 120 of them and a worse lot of brigands I never saw. Some were armed with spears, some with swords, some with knives, some with coal oil cans. They had plowed through the jungle barefooted and with few clothes because the government had ordered it and also because this particular tiger had two nights before carried off one of the villagers.

As they assembled, Captain Ahmed and Datok Shat harangued the crowd and gave them the devil for letting the tiger slip through them. They ordered another drive at once and this time, as I knew what it was all about, we took Laura along. However, she brought us no luck, for not a thing came out of the jungle except our bunch of brigands.

A third drive produced only a wa-wa monkey and as all hands were hot, tired and soaked by a shower, we went back to the rest house for a hot bath and dinner. Both were wonderful.

Our hosts were chagrined to the core and spent most of the night telephoning all over Johore for news of another tiger. Finally, they located tracks, twenty-four hours old, at Ayer Ritam about thirty miles from Batu Pahat. This seemed the best bet so the next morning we motored there and started the first drive about 9 a.m. I never was so hot in all my life as I stood in the boiling sun waiting for the tiger to

"Around the whole field was a barbed wire fence and thirty feet distant was a second fence to keep the crowd back."

come. Nothing came out and we tried another. In this, two sambar deer, a buck, and a doe broke back through the beaters and were shot, but we saw nothing.

It was all over and no tiger, so we motored back to Singapore - full of grief - to board the ship. We sailed on May 2nd at 9 a.m. and the following morning pulled into Penang (May 3rd) on the high tide at 10:30 a.m. It took all of the high tide to get us over the bar as we drew thirty feet six inches and there was only thirty-one feet on the bar at the top of high water. We were dragging mud badly.

As we were leaving the "Wilson" here and disembarking all our luggage, I had to spend most of the morning at the police station in order to obtain permission to land my guns. After these formalities were over we put up at the Runnymede Hotel and were pleased beyond measure to find such a delightful, cool, clean place. Our rooms were cool and airy and faced the harbor across a lovely lawn. During the afternoon, Laura discovered in the paper that a boat was going directly from Colombo (Ceylon) to Mombasa (Kenya) so this called for a quick shift of plans and before night we had cut out Bombay and booked on the "Mexico Maru." It saved a lot of rail travel in India, which at this time of year was said to be frightful. The "Wilson" sailed the next day at 9:30 a.m. and it was very sad to part with all our friends. We had time to see something of Penang and there was quite a lot to see at the Snake Temple and the Zoological Gardens.

We loafed over Sunday and after tiffin on Monday took a car for the sixty-four mile ride to Alor Star. About thirty miles out of Penang we ran out of the rubber and coconut plantations and into the flat lands, where every inch of the country is cultivated for rice. Alor Star is the capital of Kedah, and with a native population of about 12,000 souls, boasts a European population of sixteen families, all of whom are connected with the government.

The lawn alongside the residence of the British advisor to Kedah had been set aside for the eclipse expeditions. The British expedition had been there since March and they had set up most elaborate apparatus, thirty-eight foot cameras, etc. A small part of the field was set aside for the Harvard Eclipse Expedition and here Dr. Harlan Stetson already had erected nipa palm shelters covering the equatorial mounting and the other instruments that were to be operated by his helpers, Arnold and Johnson. Around the whole field was a barbed wire fence and thirty feet distant was a second fence to keep the crowd back so the scientists could work undisturbed. The usefulness of this double-fence arrangement, with soldiers guarding the space

Mr. and Mrs. Weld Arnold at the illuminometer were members of the Harvard Solar Eclipse Expedition of 1929.

between, was evident on the day of the eclipse when the crowds of Malays swarmed onto the field. We arrived at Alor Star about 5 p.m. on May 6th and were given a warm welcome by Judge and Mrs. Dinsmore, to whose home we had been assigned by the British advisor. As there was no hotel in the town, the European residents had generously offered to put up the various members of the British and American expeditions. Stetson, Laura and I were quartered with the judge and no more charming host could be found in all Malaya.

At 6 a.m. on May 7th I began to realize that sun shooting was not all play, for Stetson hauled me out of bed to work at the field. All the other scientific instruments were easily erected but it was quite a problem to set up cameras designed to photograph animals so they would panoram and tilt at just the right speed to follow the sun. We worked at it all day and at night were still beaten. So we went home to study it. After lengthy discussions over several glasses of beer, we decided to put three of my cameras on the equatorial mounting and let the clockwork of this machine keep them fixed on the sun as it moved through the heavens.

Bright and early next morning we were at this job, and before noon had them finally mounted, after overcoming innumerable minor obstacles of balance, etc. We had a rehearsal at 6 p.m. and in trying to rely on the British expedition's count of the seconds, I got all mixed up and did all the wrong things at the wrong time.

After totality, a counter shouted out each second on the tick of a metronome. Someone in the camp did something on each count of the 299 seconds during which totality lasted and each one had a schedule before him of when he operated. However, with the noise of the motion picture Akeley camera motor buzzing in my ear, I could not distinguish between the numbers called and so was completely confused in what I was to do next. Besides, our program was too ambitious. There were too many exposures to be made and, as plates had to be changed most carefully so as not to jar the delicate mechanism of the driving head, we had not allowed enough time between. However, the cameras worked and we went home satisfied that our program could not be simplified.

We had been bidden to the residency to a formal dinner to meet the high commissioner, Sir Hugh Clifford and his wife. All I knew about him was that he had written a lot of books of which I remember only one, *The Further Side of Silence.* I was horrified at the thought of putting on a boiled shirt and a black dinner coat while the thermometer lurked around 95 degrees. However, it had to be done, for

High cirrus clouds probably destroyed most of the scientific value of the show, but it did not prevent Prentiss and the Harvard University Expedition from seeing and photographing the most awe-inspiring spectacle that nature produces.

it was like a royal command. It was, after all, not so bad as the scene was colorful and I only lost 25 cents (Straits cents) to the high commissioner at bridge. We had at dinner the following:

Sir Hugh Clifford	High Commissioner
Lady Clifford	
T. W. Clayton	The British Advisor
Tunku Ibrahim	Son of the Sultan - The Regent
Tunku Mahmud	Brother of the Sultan
Tunku Mansur	Son of the Sultan
Tuan Mansur Aljaffri	Chief Malay Judge
Mr. & Mrs. Jackson	Leader of British Eclipse Expedition
Mr. & Mrs. Weld Arnold	Harvard Eclipse Expedition

12 British officials and A.D.C.'s.

Altogether there were twenty-four of us and after a lengthy dinner when the health of the King and the Sultan had been drunk, Sir Hugh proposed the health of President Hoover and we all drank it deeply in rare old port.

We returned at about midnight after Lady Clifford decided she could not get back from the Malayans the $40 she had lost at poker. However, films had to be loaded as this was the coolest time of the day and so it was after 3 a.m. before I turned in. Up again at 5 a.m. we were soon off to the field to watch the dawn anxiously. As it became light we saw a sky covered with clouds and then we started praying.

Our rehearsals of the morning went better as we had decided to forget the British count and rely on a timing clock of our own. At 9:30 a.m. we returned for breakfast and were greeted with a real American breakfast of puffed rice, eggs, baked beans and coffee.

Alor Star had been a quiet little place on the previous day but by this morning all pretense that all was as usual was cast aside and a pilgrimage from the country-side began to the grounds of the residency. It looked as if the natives thought the eclipse could not be seen from any other spot than our field, for very early they were lined twenty deep against our outer barbed wire fence, and the soldiers were having all they could do to keep them from swarming onto the field. There were Malays in gorgeous costumes. There were coolies with no clothes above the waist and not much below. The Sultan himself arrived and was led into the Holy of Holies within

"I was too busy during the eclipse to see much of it except on the ground glass of the cameras, but I looked up once during the long exposures and got a tremendous thrill."

the wire enclosure and given a chair, with a strong guard standing by to see that he did nothing unusual, as he was crazy as a loon.

For the next hour everybody was on tip-toe - the last tuning up of instruments - the last inspection of all the gear that had been taken weeks to erect and would be used less than five minutes. Anxious looks were cast at the sky and when on the ground a shadow cast by the sun could be detected, everyone was immediately cheered up. It's wonderful how much hope there is in the human breast. I had gone out of my way only sixty-four miles to do this job, but Stetson had to travel more than 25,000 miles before he could deliver his precious plates at home. Still, he was cheerful and appeared confident the sky would clear. An hour before the eclipse started it looked as if we should not expose a plate. At 12:09 p.m. the moon began to eat into the sun and a loud voice shouted, "First contact."

That was the signal to start and my job was to take eight pictures every ten seconds with the Akeley motion picture camera at F 4.5 with a red F filter. For an hour and twenty minutes I ground away until two and a half minutes before totality, which occurred at 1:36 p.m. local time, and then I changed film and switched on the motor of the Akeley. At the exact instant of totality with the start of the count I opened the diaphragm to F 7.7 and took off the red filter. The Akeley was then left to run by itself, giving constant exposures of 1/10 of a second for the next nine minutes. Meanwhile, Stetson operated the Soho camera with the 24-inch lens with K 1 filter at F 5.6 and I worked the duplex still picture camera with an F filter at F 14, giving exposures on both of 60 seconds, 30 seconds, and 10 seconds. Then I took off the red filter and substituted a K 1 filter and exposed 10 seconds, 5 seconds, 2 seconds.

By this time the 299 seconds, or practically five minutes, had gone and with the first ray of light that shot out as the moon moved off, we replaced the red filter on the Akeley and closed the diaphragm to F 4.5 again. During the partial phases, heavy clouds had at times shut out the sun entirely but with the approach of totality, conditions improved so that by 1:15 p.m. we had high cirrus clouds, which probably destroyed most of the scientific value of the show, but did not prevent us from seeing and photographing the most awe-inspiring spectacle that nature produces.

The soldiers had cautioned the crowd in both English and Malay to make no noise, but, as the sun diminished to a thin crescent, a hum of excitement arose. As the last bright line was extinguished, a muffled roar broke out that even the frantic

The market at Kandy was a busy place. Prentiss and Laura thought it was a gem.

waving of the soldiers could not quiet. We all felt we were taking part in some rite, mystical and awful. An explosion of firecrackers by Chinese to scare away the dragon that was swallowing the sun made me think of how the people of ancient times must have felt when the sun, sometimes their god, disappeared with no assurance from their priests that it would ever appear again. All they could realize would be growing dusk, the gradual cutting down of the sun and finally its complete disappearance and darkness over the face of the land. What could the poor people think but that some dragon had swallowed it up because of the sins committed by man, or because God was angry?

I was too busy during the eclipse to see much of it except on the ground glass of the cameras, but I looked up once during the long exposures and got a tremendous thrill. Strange to my mind also was the fact that the stars were out in the middle of the day.

As the sun burst forth again triumphant, I began the grind of taking eight pictures every ten seconds for another hour and a half, and by 3 p.m. when it was all over I was fed up with the job and fully ready to go home to tiffin. A good hour's rest and we were back at the field packing up, for we were to leave in the morning for Penang.

About noon on May 10th we left Alor Star in two motors and reached Penang about 3 p.m. The bugless comfort of the Runnymede Hotel was most welcome for I have never seen a place where so much big game flew about after dark as at Alor Star.

The next day we were aboard the steamer "Malayan Prince" at noon and settled down to four days of quiet and comfort on our way to Colombo.

About noon on May 15th our ship was off the breakwater of Colombo but it was three hours before we had taken aboard our pilot, passed through the narrow entrance into a small harbor crowded with boats, and made fast to our moorings.

The doctor was slow in arriving so the day was about over when we arrived at the Galle Face Hotel. This was a delightful hotel close by the sea with the surf veritably breaking in the garden. Our rooms were comfortable and the food good.

The next morning we were away early by auto to Kandy, seventy two miles back in the hills. The road led through a succession of rice paddies, coconut and rubber plantations and finally, as the higher elevation of 1,600 feet was reached, through the tea estates.

Native life along the road, including a work elephant and master, were new sights for the world travelers.

The view down the narrow gorges of the river hemmed in by densely wooded hills was inspiring. The native life along the road, the bullock carts, the elephants bearing heavy burdens, all were new and strange. Natives cultivating the rice paddies, knee-deep in mud wielding a heavy hoe that did duty as both pick and shovel, were here before us in the flesh just as we had read and seen pictured in books. Some of the larger owners had a water buffalo to drag a rude wooden plow while man and beast sweated at the effort of pulling their feet out of the sticky clay.

Kandy was a gem, surrounding a little lake and nestling among the hills. We lunched on the veranda of the Suisse Hotel just across from the Temple of the Tooth, which rose on many terraces until its multicolored buildings were lost in the dense foliage of the hillside.

A trip to Katugastota to see the work elephants bathing, and a run around the Botanical Gardens at Peradeniya left us barely enough time for the three-hour run back to Colombo. Automobiling in all of these countries was distinctly unpleasant to me. In the Straits Settlements I was terrified at the speed they seemed to consider normal and at the reckless driving of practically every car we met. In Ceylon they did not drive as fast but their pedestrians and the bullock carts clutter up the road every inch of the way and have no idea of giving way to let a car pass. It seemed a miracle that we did not kill a hundred natives on our 150 mile ride. Traffic was a lot worse than Fifth Avenue all the way to Kandy because it is all over the road and all moving at different speeds in any old direction.

We were greatly intrigued by the dress of the natives. Some wore full robes even pulled over their heads. Others had nothing much before and half as much behind. The Buddhist priests were in orange or yellow robes, but the tortoise-shell combs, worn like a tiara by the older Sinhalese men, amused us most.

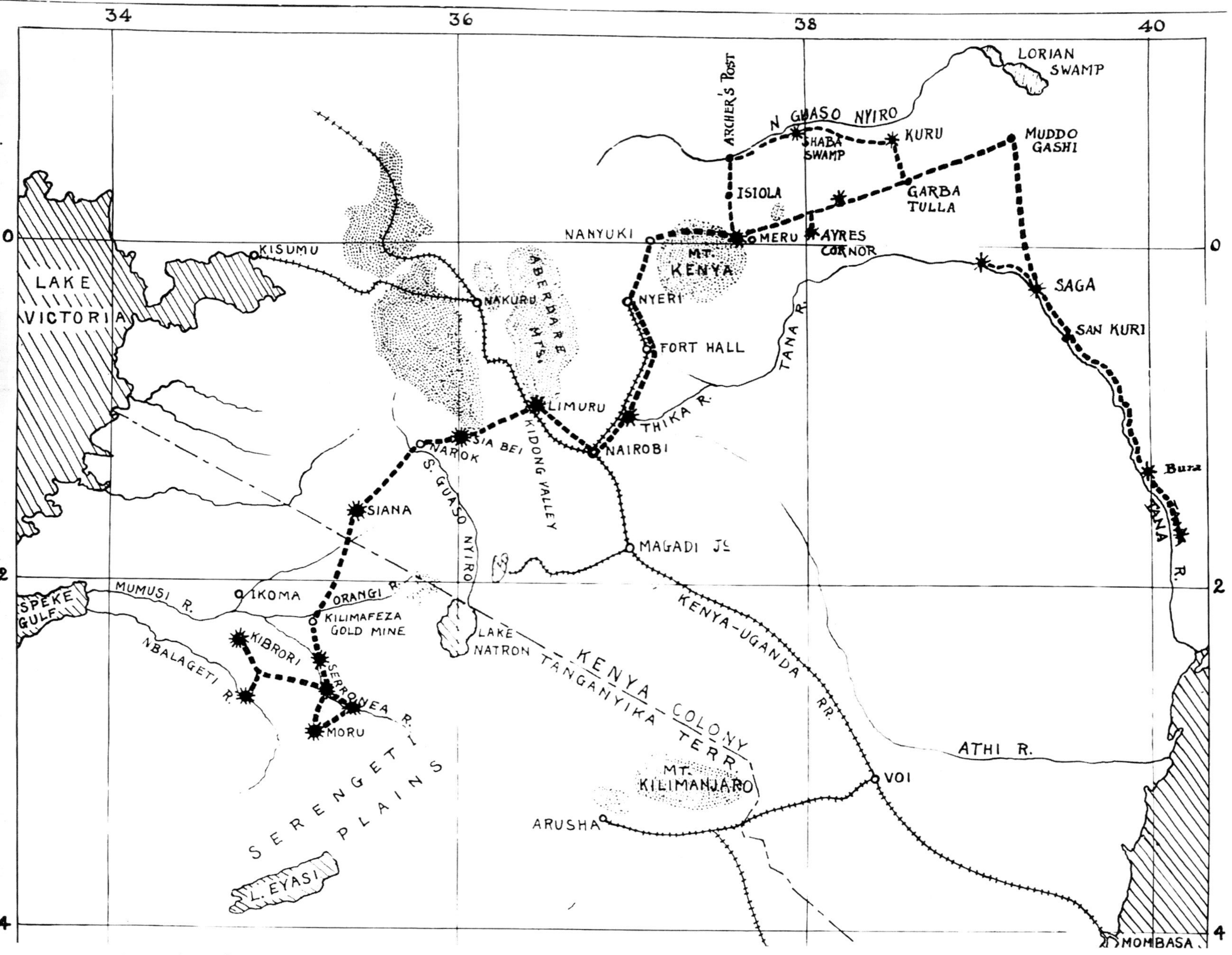

A map drawn by Prentiss N. Gray shows his travels through Kenya and Tanganyika as he and Laura crossed the Serengeti Plains in search of photographs and big game. Stars drawn on the map show where collections of specimens were made.

TANGANYIKA

PART TWO

TRACKING THE HERDS OF THE SERENGETI PLAINS

WE sailed from Colombo on the "S.S. Mexico Maru" of the Osaka Shosen Kaisha at 6 p.m. on May 18th. Then followed eleven lazy days with nothing to do and no energy to do it. The only break in the trip was passing the Maldive Islands, whose name I had seen in a stamp album but never believed they really existed. All we saw of them were low coral atolls, but a book, *The Eastern Pilot*, informed us there were 76,000 people on the string of islands ruled by a sultan who collected port dues from visiting vessels in rice, dried fish and red handkerchiefs.

After this there was nothing until we picked up land near Kilidindi, which is the port of Mombasa. We had dreaded this trip on a 5,800-ton cargo ship, but we were really very comfortable as it was the season of the southwest monsoons and we had a gentle cool breeze in our teeth the whole trip. The thermometer never rose above 86 degrees and as our cabin had two ports forward, it was even cooler there. The temperature of the water was 82 to 86 degrees all the way. The passengers were few - two other couples, Mr. and Mrs. T. A. Wood, mayor of Nairobi; Dr. and Mrs. F. J. A. Beringer; R. Noel-Paton, Dr. Gordon Chissel; and Cecil d'Oyly-John; besides the usual assortment of Indians, Chinese and Japanese who slept, ate and dressed on the afterdeck.

Our steaming speed was not all it was cracked up to be and we only picked up the pilot after our 2,570-mile trip at 1:30 p.m. on May 28th. An hour later we passed in through the reef and wound our way up the tortuous but deep harbor of Kilidindi. We dropped anchor in the stream and it was a full hour more before we

Just as Prentiss and Laura came into Stoney Athi, Kenya, they were lucky enough to see giraffe within 200 yards.

were ashore with our twenty-three pieces of luggage and passed customs. However, in all my travels I have never seen such polite and decent customs officials. It was now nip and tuck to catch the 4:30 p.m. train, but by much speeding across the island and expeditious dumping of the baggage onto the train, we were at last on board, with five minutes to spare.

We had a most comfortable compartment in a spotlessly clean corridor train. A dining car served excellent meals and, fortunately, it just had rained so much there was no dust. After dinner the porter brought in two rolls of bedding and transformed the seats into quite comfortable bunks, so that our first night ashore we really slept well.

The next morning I was awake before light with both eyes glued to the window to see the herds of game I had read so much about. However, I sat there for two solid hours before I saw a thing. Then, a small herd of Thomson's gazelle about 400 yards away caught my eye and soon we were seeing plenty of wildebeest, kongoni (Coke's hartebeest), ostriches, zebra and tommies (Thomson's gazelle). A few Grant's gazelle were distinguishable by their larger size and a lack of a black stripe along their sides.

Just as we came into Stoney Athi, we were lucky enough to see five giraffes within 200 yards. Mr. Wood, who was watching with us, told us it was the first time he had seen them from the railroad and he has lived in Kenya twenty-nine years.

We pulled into Nairobi exactly on time and found both Philip Percival and W. Wedgwood Bowen there to meet us. Soon we were settled in the Avenue Hotel, which had only been opened a few months. After lunch we pitched into the work of packing at Safariland. The next day this packing business kept up all day long and far into the night with only a stop for tea at the Muthaiga Country Club.

June 1, 1929. This whole day passed in a blue haze. There were a thousand and one things to be purchased for two months in the bush and while we were scheduled to start at noon, at 2 p.m. we were having lunch in the Avenue Hotel. However, leaving undone only the usual number of things, we were away at 2:30 p.m. in two one and one-half ton Ford trucks and one three-quarter ton Ford rebuilt as a hunting and camera car.[1]

[1] Prentiss Gray had the three-quarter ton truck fitted with two rear axles and six wheels. It was shipped from the United States to Nairobi several months before he and Laura arrived to begin their safari.

"Our safari vehicles were two one- and one- half-ton Ford trucks and one three-quarter ton Ford truck."

Our personnel consisted of W. Wedgwood Bowen, ornithologist from the Philadelphia Academy of Natural Sciences; Philip Percival, white hunter; Laura and myself; and fifteen boys. The road for the first seventeen miles was pretty bad after the hard rains so we decided to spend our first night at a little inn called the High View Hotel at Limuru, which was situated at an elevation of 7,100 feet overlooking the Nairobi Valley.

There was a thick mist over everything when we crawled our of our little wattle-and-daub cabins the next morning, and we decided to wait a bit for things to dry out before the start. We were away before 10 a.m. and in a short distance reached the eastern edge of the Great Rift Valley, elevation 7,600 feet. Before us stretched a great sink in the earth's crust that extended for 2,400 miles from South Africa across the Red Sea and up into Arabia. It was green and beautiful for we were seeing it at its best. Here and there along its sides volcanic cones showed its origin and the lava dust of the road spoke of the cause of the tremendous upheaval that had caused it. We dropped down a steep road 2,240 feet to the floor and stopped to take on water at a little stream, for we had ahead of us forty miles of waterless road. The boys found a spitting cobra near the water and Bowen shot it after it had made a vain attempt to spit its poison into his eyes.

We ran across the valley, stopping on the edge of the Masai Game Reserve to interview the game warden and make a cup of tea. We were on game all the time and herds of kongoni, tommies and zebra were on every hand. Close to the road, five giraffes stood and gazed at us before they trotted off in a lumbering gait.

We climbed the Mau Escarpment after crossing the part of the Rift called the Kedong. The pull was steep but where we reached the top it was only 6,925 feet. We dropped down a little and made our first camp of the trip at Sia Bei. It was by a lovely stream and before we knew it the tents were up and tea on the table. Two hours later we were served a splendid dinner of soup, roast chicken, fruit and cheese. We sat around the fire under a clear sky studded with stars and enjoyed our first African night out-of-doors.

We were away the next day shortly after 8 a.m. and found good going until about 1 p.m. when we stopped for lunch. While we were eating, the porters dug a road down into a donga, which would have been impossible for the cars without this work. During the afternoon we began to see plenty of game - topi, kongoni, wildebeest, giraffes, tommies, Grant's gazelle, eland and zebra. It took all the ache

"Before we knew it, the tents were up and tea on the table."

out of our bones to see this game but when we rolled into camp at 4:30 p.m., after seventy-five miles on the road, we had had enough. Here Percival had a couple of mules that he was going to try to take through the fly belt. He had previously brought down a box that was fully screened against the tsetse fly. This camp was called Sianna and it was a beautiful site overlooking vast plains where numerous game were feeding.

The next day started by one of the drivers calling, "Lion."

We rushed out but simba had trotted into the bush before we caught a glimpse of it. However, the mules got his scent and they broke their ropes and tore for the bush. It took two hours to find them and get them back, and after, we tried to get them into the box on one of the Ford trucks. It was a fine job, with much kicking and snorting, but within a half-hour we had them in and the doors locked. This was the first attempt to take riding mules into Tanganyika through the fly belt and, as it had caused no end of talk in Nairobi, we were anxious to make a success of it. We were in fly-infested country soon after we started and despite our precaution we were all bitten a number of times before the end of the day. At the end of fifty miles we pulled up at Campi Ya Nyota in a beautiful orchard bush country where thorn trees dotted the plains. We had a bite of lunch and just as we finished, a wart hog trotted by camp and I fired my first shot in Africa to drop him. We then found a convenient topi at 150 yards and knocked it over for meat for the men. We left two men to dress it out and Laura and I strolled back to camp. On the way back I shot a tommie for our table.

Percival pulled in with the mules about 4:30 p.m. and our camp was soon erected. Quite near camp was a large pile of rocks in which we found a catch basin containing water. Baboons sat up on the rocks above us and scolded us while we filled our cans. At 8 p.m. just before dinner, we heard jackals at the wart hog I had shot and we drove down there. Their eyes shone brightly in the car lights and one of the drivers shot one. Bowen shone his flashlight beyond the rim of the campfire light and picked up more shining eyes. We put on another light and there were five lions within seventy-five yards of the fire. We shuddered when we thought that our jackals might have turned out to be lions as we could see nothing of them but two shining eyes. Besides, we had gone out for the jackals with only three shells. No more night shooting with a pocket flashlight for us. Laura fairly had the wind up when she thought of lions in her bedroom. We decided it was a fool country.

W. Wedgwood Bowen, ornithologist from The Academy of Natural Sciences of Philadelphia, prepares a bird specimen.

We had not moved a mile from this camp before we located three lions just leaving a kill. We started after them in the car at once and ran them over a mile and a half but they got into a donga and as they were fairly small we decided not to take the time to drive them out. We visited the kill, a zebra, and which was, now that the lions had left it, a fighting mass of hyenas, jackals and vultures. We took some pictures, but as we approached the hyenas and jackals moved off and as we reached a point twenty yards away, the vultures quit it.

We had only forty miles to cover to our first base camp at Seronera, so we did not crowd the cars. The lorry with the mules in their fly-proof box took it particularly slowly and we passed it on the road. It was the best stretch of road we had had on the whole trip and sometimes we even got up to a comfortable speed of twenty miles an hour. However, as sure as we tried to move along at a good speed, our front wheels would drop into a pig hole or a deep rut hidden by the high grass. Most of our road for the last 150 miles had been just a wheel track across the plains or twisting through the scrub. Wherever the soil was soft it was worn into deep ruts, which you could not possibly run in without tearing off all your under body. Most of it was hidden in grass three feet high so you really had no idea where you were going.

About noon we pulled into the Seronera camp, a lovely bit of open woods set in the middle of the vast Tanganyika Plains. There was a small stream, the headwaters of the Seronera River, but it now carried but little water and only dirty pools told that in the rainy season it was a rushing torrent.

As we pulled up with our car, a large lioness broke out of the donga and trotted into the brush on the far side. Everyone was wild with excitement. We hesitated between taking after it with a gun or setting up the cameras, but long before we had decided which to do, the lioness had quietly moved into high grass and was out of sight. Camp for the next half-hour hummed with conversation as to how we could find the lioness again. Percival, meanwhile, sat back serenely and smiled secretly, knowing that each day he could fill our eyes with cats until we cried for a change of scenery.

Certainly the plains are swarming with game. We could see thousands of head from camp of zebra, topi, tommies and kongoni. Laura and I had a 10 by 12 foot tent with four and a half foot walls. A fly over all extended six feet in front as a porch and six feet behind as a bathroom. We slept on broad cots with air mat-

Masai warriors

tresses, our arctic robes over this, then sheets and a jaeger blanket. A proper table and chairs completed our equipment, plus a bathtub and wash basin.

Our tent boy, Hassan, just sat about waiting for Laura to order something and soon he knew more about her underclothing and what to lay out for her than she did. He did all the washing and made up the tent, besides bringing us tea and sundowners.

I had a gun boy named Kimoni who had never been known to smile and looked it. I was right glad of that for, when he witnessed some of my shooting, he otherwise might have burst into glee. Percival had his tent on one side of us and Bowen on the other, which was a great comfort. Somebody else would be chewed before the lion reached our tent.

The fifteen boys, cook, gun boys and porters were grouped about the kitchen twenty-five yards away in little tents made of americani, or heavy white cotton cloth. The mules were tethered just before our tent and four of the dogs were penned up nearby while two roamed loose to give the alarm in case anything came too near. We were comfortable, clean, even luxurious. We had passed through 100 miles of fly country without getting sleeping sickness, so we were happy.

We started off after an early breakfast to reconnoiter the country. Percival, Laura, a gunbearer, native driver and myself, and all the guns and cameras, made quite a load for the camera car. We saw literally thousands of wildebeest, zebra and tommies, for wherever we looked across the plain they dotted the landscape to the horizon. We drove slowly along all the dongas in the hopes of putting up a lion and about 11 a.m., out of a small patch of brush, popped a lioness and a cub about eighteen months old. We gave chase in the car with the cameras ready and after about a mile the lioness had outstripped the cub. The cub was visibly tired. The lion pulled up and made a great display of tail lashing and growling. We took a little film. It was lying down in grass two feet high. There was little to be photographed except round ears and a busy tail, so we went off and left it.

A half-hour later we put three lionesses and a lion out of a patch of brush and they galloped off across the plain. We drove after them and after a mile and a half one of the lionesses lay down. We moved up to seventy yards and took quite a little film, but when I raised up above the cab of the car with my still camera, the lioness became furious and gave every appearance of charging, so we left.

Two natives who had been looking after the dogs before our arrival, had been

They heard a roar, the dogs scattered, and over the top of the rock scrambled a lioness.

badly scared by a pair of lions. They thought they made their home in a pile of rocks and since our arrival had begged Percival to drive this cover. After lunch we decided to try it so took a half dozen boys and five dogs. Laura sat in the car while we urged the dogs in. Soon we heard a roar, the dogs scattered, and over the top of the rock scrambled a lioness. Soon the dogs located it again and the lioness broke cover with the dogs close behind it. When the lioness left the rocks for the open plain it stopped and let the dogs come in close. It took after one of them and was off again with the other four at its heels. Percival yelled to me to kill the lioness before it cleaned up all the dogs. I fired and the lioness went down only to get to its feet again and take after another dog that it evidently blamed for its hurt. A second shot put the lioness down for good. We came up to find the first shot had broken the lioness' rear leg and ranged forward. The second had torn its heart and lungs badly. It was dead when we arrived and the dogs, including the one the lioness had mauled, were having a grand worry at it. The lioness weighed 360 pounds.

It was a wonderful thrill, for there were anxious moments after the dogs found the lioness till it came out roaring. There were more anxious moments after the lioness was hit as to which way it was going, and the final joy when it went down.

Daylight the next morning found us cruising over the veldt till we spotted five lions on top of a grassy rise looking at us. They were a half mile away so we slowly started toward them. When we came up to the spot where they had been, we saw them slowly working toward a donga. There was one old male and four lionesses and, at about 200 yards, just at the edge of the donga, the lion turned on us, lashing his tail and grunting in the most approved style. We felt the male lion was of no use as a photographic subject so we moved off. A little later Percival spotted a lioness out in the open lying on an ant hill. We approached slowly and found it was a splendid tempered old girl that was torn between a desire to go to sleep and a slight curiosity as to what we were. We began taking film at seventy yards and slowly moved up to just twenty yards. There we sat for an hour while I exposed every foot of film we had in the car.

The lioness lay on its ant hill and yawned, licked itself, and gazed at the herds of game on the plains. Finally, the lioness stood up and stretched and then walked past our car not three feet from the radiator to the edge of the donga where it sat on its haunches like a dog and regarded us. After five minutes, the lioness sauntered back and took up its position on the ant hill where we left the lioness.

Percival spotted a lioness out in the open lying on an ant hill.

A Grant's gazelle hardly hit the ground from the top of Prent's car
before three lionesses were on it as if they had never seen a square meal.

On the way home about noon we saw a Robert's gazelle with a good head so I left the car and stalked it. The second shot brought it down. The gazelle proved to have a splendid head, which measured a spread of 29-3/8 inches and a length along the horn of 23-1/2 inches.

We decided not to hunt in the afternoon as I had to make a gun rack for the car and rig up the flashlight camera. Percival shot a zebra for bait for this camera and we never had a minute's peace all evening until the carcass was finished. We had placed it 400 yards from camp and the hyenas succeeded in breaking the trip wire of the camera without putting off the flash. Then there was a free-for-all fight over the carcass. As I was sitting up late loading film, I got the full benefit of it while the rest of the camp slept at intervals. Whenever the hyenas and jackals on the kill let up for a few minutes, our dogs in camp took it up, venturing as far out as they dared. They finally stirred up a lion and came home yelping and barking. They scared me out of a year's growth as they came tearing through the long grass right up to me, where I was working with my hands in a changing bag in front of our tent. I was sure they were bringing the lion with them and I was torn between pulling my hands out of the bag to grab a gun and risk flashing the film I was changing, or sitting still and letting the lion eat the film and myself.

Our first two hours hunting the next morning drew blank. Then we saw three lionesses and worked around to look them over. When we reached a point sixty yards from the nearest one, we stopped to ascertain its disposition. Two had moved on perhaps a hundred yards ahead but as soon as we stopped they turned and walked straight back to us. One sat down fifty yards away but the other came on until the lioness was not move than ten yards from the radiator. The lioness walked completely around the car and looked us all over, then yawned and went off twenty-five yards and lay down.

We took this occasion to slip away to shoot something on which they could feed. In half an hour we were back with a Grant's gazelle on the top of our car and, as we drove close to them, I pushed it off. It had hardly hit the ground before all three lionesses were on it and tearing and eating as if they had never seen a square meal before. We drove off a little way till they had really settled down to the free feed and then back we came to a position about twenty yards away. From here we took a thousand feet of film and four dozen stills without the animals paying us the slightest bit of attention.

The Serengeti Plains teemed with game, including thousands of kongoni.

Finally, they had disposed of everything except the horns and some of the skeleton and one by one they left. The last one to leave looked back when the lioness had gone a short distance and saw the vultures, which had been gathering in the sky, dropping down to what was left of the kill. This did not please the lioness at all and back it came, putting the vultures at a respectable distance again. The lioness picked up the skull and backbone, which was all that was left of the Grant's gazelle, and carried it away. The lioness was not leaving even a free smell for the birds.

As we drove away we found that our three lionesses had joined six more that, up to this time, had been concealed in the long grass along the donga. Among these was a cub that appeared more afraid of us than the old ones. We headed home feeling as if we had done a full day's work, for this photographing lions as near as you get in a zoo but with no bars between is nervous work and we were all pretty tired.

We met two Masai hunters as we drove back to camp who were short on raiment but long on ornament. They also had a surplus of red clay rubbed into their hair.

I spent the evening until midnight loading film but just before I turned in, I sat for half an hour before the tent and listened to the noises of the African night, which are one of the most interesting features of a safari.

After the tropic night has fallen suddenly, a myriad of sounds come to you telling of life in the animal world that is a hundred times more active in darkness than in daylight; the howl of a hyena; the yapping of jackals; the deep "boom" of an ostrich; a zebra barks and then the thunderous beat of hoofs tell that the herd has stampeded from their enemy, the lion; a thousand wildebeest croak like frogs in a swamp all about the camp; a deep vibration rather than a sound strikes your ears and you know that a lion has started on it hunt. The sound gradually grows louder as it comes nearer until a series of grunts from deep in the lion's chest tells you it is looking over your camp at close range.

Perhaps out beyond the range of the light of the campfire you see two balls of fire gleaming and try to guess from their distance apart whether they are the eyes of a jackal, hyena or old simba himself. You laugh foolishly and get off some banality about turning in. What you really do, as soon as you reach your tent, is to look into the magazine of your rifle to be sure it contains five shells. You put them there yourself, not an hour before. With the gun where you can grab it with one movement, you securely tuck in the mosquito net over your bed, leaving not a single hole

For an hour Percival argued with Masai warriors before he could get around to asking them about lion and other game.

through which a lion could crawl. With this security you are asleep in a moment.

The next morning we drove down the donga through a parklike country that was as nearly typical of the Africa of hunting books as you could imagine. After about a mile we put up three lions but they had no faith in the publicity value of the movies and did not wait for us. We started to try to round them up but dropped our front wheels over a big log in the grass and hung up. It took a half-hour's work to get clear and by that time the lions had vamoosed. We drove out across the plains to a rounded hill from which we could see miles in every direction. In the distance rose brushy hills and stretching from us to their base was the great Serengeti Plains. Tremendous herds of game dotted it in every direction. The wildebeest stood out as black dots or as black splashes in the close-packed herds. The zebra at this distance were grey while the topi and kongoni were reddish. In between were thousands of tommies and Grant's gazelle, their little white tails flashing in the brilliant sunlight.

It was the sort of thing one's forefathers looked upon before the millions of buffalo and pronghorn were wiped off the great American plains. The same depletion of game as America experienced will occur here as the country is fenced and settled, and before we die we will be able to boast of having seen it.

We had a beat for lion in the afternoon, putting the porters and the dogs through a series of rock piles that stuck up in the plain. We got nothing out but several dik-dik; the dogs killed a silver jackal down a hole. On the way home we met a lioness coming out of the only rock pile we had not beaten. However, we were looking for a maned lion and did not bother the lioness.

We hunted to the north the next day to find the tail of the wildebeest migration. About 11 a.m. we came up with it and none of us, not even Percival, had ever seen anything like it. How many beasts were in sight no human could estimate. All we could say was that as far as the eye could see in every direction the plain teemed with wildebeest. Here and there a herd of zebra, topi or kongoni were mixed in with the black beasts. Dust rose in clouds as suddenly as a herd took a notion to move. For the photographer, it was hopeless. No picture could be taken to give an adequate idea of the immensity of these herds. We tried our best, feeling that our efforts were feeble. We moved in and out among the herds for a couple of hours trying to estimate their numbers and watching their antics.

About noon we moved into orchard bush country in a low range of hills. Here

Masai women watch the exchange between Percival and the warriors.

we found a waterbuck that I shot. Its horns measured 25-3/8 inches in length. We returned to camp at 2 p.m. and I put in the rest of the afternoon developing test films until it was time to go out and kill a wildebeest as bait for our flashlight camera. The two nights it had fired had produced two hyena pictures but we were hopeful a lion would come to the kill before long.

Then came a bad day. We had driven out to hunt in brush country. We reached a pile of rocks about ten miles from camp and a couple of klipspringers appeared near the top. I missed my first shot but the second drew blood. Then followed a two-hour chase on the trail without any result, for we finally lost it in a tangle of rocks and thorns that we could not get through. We drove on about a mile when a leopard leaped out of a tree and started across the open. I jumped over the side of the truck and lit hard on one heel, breaking both bones just above the ankle. I went down in a heap as it hurt a lot, and the leopard sauntered off smiling. An hour later we tried to drive the patch of brush he had entered but without results. My left foot was out of business completely, but with it propped up I could still sit in the car. About 5 p.m. we reached camp where soon we had the leg properly set in a plaster cast and with a pair of homemade crutches I could get about.

Percival, meanwhile, started to fix the three-quarter ton truck and dropped the body on his left hand smashing it badly.

We were a very sad crew the next morning - Percival with a smashed hand; my foot completely out of business; and the three-quarter ton truck with a busted rear spring.

Some days later we drove the big rocks near camp in the hope of putting out a lion but no result. Then we tried a nearby donga and in a few minutes put up a leopard. The leopard jumped into the crotch of a tree and I knocked it out with a shot. Then the five dogs closed in and there was a hell of a row, which ended in successive yelps as one after another of the dogs were put out of the fight. Just at the end the leopard ran up a tree and Percival fired three charges of buckshot into it at forty yards. The dogs refused to go in again as it appeared one dog had an eye out, one was bitten through the chest, one through the hind leg and the other two somewhat scratched. We drove back to camp for the little car so we could get close to where the leopard lay in the high grass. We finally brought it up, broken spring and all, and drove it within ten feet of where we supposed the leopard lay. We searched the grass by firing shotgun shells into it and just as we were about to give

A migration of wildebeest passed. The lions followed, and so did the men.

it up one of our porters up a tree yelled he had seen the leopard slip into a patch of short grass not far away. This patch was fifty feet from the donga and was not more than ten by twenty feet in area. We drove the car through it one way and turned and drove through it the other. The leopard emerged from between our rear wheels and bolted into the donga before we could get a shot. That was the last we ever saw of it and we returned to camp sore at heart.

As we were searching the plains the next day for lion we met five Masai warriors all decked out with spears and shields. They had very little on, only a bit of rag that mostly was draped about their shoulders, but their ears and hair were full of adornment. For an hour Percival argued with them about everything in the world before he could get around to asking them about lion and other game. Finally, they allowed that the place where they had just come from crawled with lion and rhino, and after another hour Percival arranged that they should return and guide us for five shillings a day for all five of them.

We drove two of them back to camp with us and they sat about in amazement while we struck camp. Never had they seen such a lot of impedimenta, as the Masai way of traveling was to take a spear and shield and some pieces of meat on a stick like a brochette. That was all he needed and thereby he had it on us a mile.

We shifted camp fifteen miles to the range of hills on the western side of the plains, which are sometimes called the Masai Steppes. Here we found a Masai village of about twenty huts. They had fully a thousand head of cattle, which were divided up in five or six herds tended by the small boys. The warriors did nothing but strut about with their spears while the women drew the water and carried the wood. The elders came formally to call on us as soon as we made camp and brought some milk for us, which we let the men have as it did not look very sanitary.

All the Masai men wore only a single piece of cloth draped from the shoulder, which sometimes hung down in front or more often was put back out of the way around their neck. Everyone was daubed from head to foot in a mixture of mutton tallow and red ochre so that they appeared copper colored and not black. Their hair was filled with it and the height of their ambition seemed to be to have at least one big pigtail.

Their houses, built in an oval inside a thorn boma, were about four feet high with one low round entrance through which they could crawl. They were constructed of sticks plastered over with cow dung. At night all the cattle were driven inside the

Zebra pass through a thicket.

boma and the center soon became a mass of filth. Flies swarmed everywhere in indescribable number. The women were not much to look at except their neck decorations of rings of wire were at least novel.

We started hunting before daylight in the big truck with our usual gunbearers and four Masai who were to show us hundreds of maned lions. We searched every donga but never saw a single sign, to the great discomfiture of the Masai who had promised great things. About 10 a.m. we saw a good reed buck and I fired a whole bunch of shells at it without the least damage. Then I tried to kill a hyena and the result was even more lamentable. Next we tried to get a tommie for the camp but neither Percival nor I could hit one. We were both off our shooting and so far it was laughable. Finally I gave up and Percival managed in ten shots to kill a Grant's gazelle so we had meat in camp. Just then out jumped a leopard and we tried to get it before it reached the donga with no better result. We came back to camp.

The Masai were on hand before daylight and by 6:30 a.m. we had found a very good bushbuck, which I was lucky enough to drop in his tracks with one shot. As it was only a short way from camp, we sent it back to the skinner and as soon as the truck returned, moved on up the donga. We soon made out five lions stealing off through the grass headed for cover. They proved to be two males with only small manes and three lionesses, and as we did not wish to shoot any of these we tried to approach for their pictures. This, however, they resented and slipped to cover.

We began to notice that the plains were deserted by the wildebeest. No matter where we drove only a few small herds were in evidence. The night before countless thousands were everywhere about us and now they had gone. There was only one conclusion. The tail of the migration had passed on. That meant the lions would follow the migration and we must do likewise. We, therefore, cut the morning hunt short and returned to camp to order a move. Bowen was heartbroken as he was in a paradise of nesting birds and getting some splendid stuff for his collection. So he decided to spend a few days more in this camp and we would send back for him.

Here he had met for the first time Leopold's go-away bird, a noisy but wary species, dull grayish above with a naked black face, long brown crest and a white throat washed with green in the region of the crop. Yellow shouldered parrots with green underparts and blue rumps, orange-headed lovebirds with green bodies and bluish tails, and lilac-throated rollers with long tails and bright blue underparts lent

A Ndorobo hunter of the Wadorobo tribe takes aim.

color to the scene. In the breeding season, the roller performs aerial revolutions unsurpassed by the aces of modern aviation. Nose dives, corkscrews, loops and all such stunts form part of the display, which is always accompanied by deep-voiced grating calls.

Superb glossy starlings with glossy green backs and chestnut bellies flew about in small flocks from tree to tree whistling shrilly. Dull-colored mouse-birds crept amidst the thicker foliage, often hanging upside down, their long tails pointing almost vertically upwards. The ubiquitous bulbul, a dull bird save for a patch of bright yellow under the tail, was as usual common, and its cheerful little song was often to be heard. Wood-hoopoes with long tails, dark purple and greenish-glossed bodies and long curved red bills, played follow-my-leader about the tree trunks in search of insects.

At a water hole in the mornings between 8 and 9 a.m. yellow-throated sandgrouse came to drink, flying in small flocks and parties, always uttering their characteristic call of "gruk-glock, gruk-glock." These birds lie in the open plains during the heat of the day, sunning and dusting themselves, and come to drink as regularly as clock-work once each day. They often fly many miles to quench their thirst.

Of game birds there were bare-throated francolins, whose harsh cacklings were often heard, particularly in the early mornings and late afternoon; helmeted guinea fowl; and the Cape quail.

Three species of bustard roamed the open plains. The largest, the Somali kori, stands about three feet high. These birds are probably the largest flying birds (Ostriches do not fly). The other two species are both quite small and one, the least common of the two in that region, may be distinguished by the black belly of the male.

The avifauna of the plains was composed mostly of larks and coursers. Of the former family there were many species. Flappet larks hovered overhead clapping their wings and producing a sound as loud as that made by clapping human hands together. Finch larks were abundant and fed in small parties and flocks upon the bare ground.

In the long grass near the Seronera River, dainty grass-warblers were busy feeding their young, that were housed in frail baskets of woven grass. In the trees and undergrowth along the banks of the river, honey guides chattered and invited one to follow in search of honey. Occasionally, parties of helmeted shrikes appeared,

Lions selected choice morsels of a kill and dragged it under a tree.

chattering and clapping their bills at the intruder. Along the stony bed of dried-up portion of the Seronera River, numerous nightjars rested during the day, coming out at dusk to hawk for insects, or to disturb the night with their monotonous "churring." Bowen collected one new species of sandgrouse that he named *Nyctiperdix decoratus katharinae.*

We had not gone far in our packing before the Masai became aware we were leaving. The whole village arrived to gather up any leftover tins or discarded rope or cloth. We had a chance to look all the village belles over again but I did not see anything to make us alter our plan of leaving.

We traveled just twenty miles in a northwest direction and camped on the Seronera River, which flows into the Gurumeti. We picked up the migration and once more the plain was alive with game. Clouds of dust arose everywhere as the foolish wildebeest tore about in play or simulated fright.

While the boys were pitching camp, we took a turn around and about a mile above camp saw a yellow head with two round ears rise above the grass. We stopped thirty yards away and watched. Another head popped up and another and another till we thought they had us surrounded. We counted eight young lions and lionesses within fifty yards. We drew off as the light was too bad to photograph, and going off half a mile, shot a wildebeest and dragged it back for their supper. Our theory was that if well fed they might stay in the donga all night and not go wandering off. Then they would be available for pictures in the morning.

We dragged the kill behind the car across their front and dropped it not far off. It took them some time to realize our generosity, but finally an old lioness trusted its nose and came out to see. The lioness fell to with vigor and the sound of its gobbling started the rest out of the brush. As they trooped out we counted twelve and two cubs. Not a shootable head in the bunch so they were destined for pictures. We regretted, when we saw the size of the bunch, that we had not provided more dinner for them, but as it was getting dark we started back to camp full of hope for the morning.

We were up at 4:30 a.m. and with the first crack of dawn started the cars. Our ungrateful guests of the night before had licked the platter clean and departed. We drove all over the country, looked into every bit of cover, but never saw a sign of them. We were mad clear through at the ungrateful wretches. After a long hunt, seeing hundreds of thousands of wildebeest, tommies, and Grant's gazelle, but nothing we wanted to shoot, we picked up a topi for meat.

On the way back to camp, after the light had gone photographically, we saw three lions on a kill. They had about polished it off except for a few choice morsels, which they had dragged off under a tree. The vultures, two hyenas, and numerous jackals were sitting about the cleaned skeleton, but at a distance that the lions considered respectful. The moment one approached nearer, one of the lions would make a short charge and everything would scatter. We hoped they might serve as studies later so killed them a wildebeest a quarter of a mile away. At the shot they fled to the donga but when we dragged the kill near them, we could see three round heads with round ears watching us, so we had no fear they would not find it.

Somehow this did not seem like Africa. Often in the morning when we drove off I had on the same hunting suit I wore in Canada and Wyoming, plus a sweater and a leather jacket. I seldom took them off till nearly 10 a.m. When we sat down to dinner at night I found great comfort in my eider-down coat.

The following day, not a mile from camp, we found our troop of fourteen lions but they were lying down in cover and it was a problem how to get at them. We drove off, killed a wildebeest, and dragged it into a favorable position, out in the open and not far from where they lay. Then we waited but they did not come out from cover and after two hours we decided to return to camp for something to read while waiting for their appetites to return.

We were only away twenty minutes but on our return found eight full-grown lions and two cubs fighting and snarling and fairly groveling in the kill. We drove to within thirty yards and began taking pictures of this struggling, writhing mass. Nearby, under the shade of the little trees, sat four more full-grown lions. There was not a maned head in the bunch so we devoted all our thoughts to photography. During the next three hours we were within forty yards of them all the time and as close as ten yards to some. We ground off 1,100 feet of film and six dozen stills, and at 1 p.m. started back to camp utterly worn out. At least, I was thinking of focus and exposure. Laura actually sat in the back of the car and embroidered and Percival sat in front with his gun out the window and read the *Saturday Evening Post.* That's how exciting this lion picture business is after the first nervous few minutes when you are moving in on them and don't know how they are going to take your visit. There was never a moment when one showed any marked annoyance at us. Twice they dragged the kill a little farther away when we came too near and several times they snarled at us, but that's not half what some of the cross old members of the troop meted out to the smaller ones when the younger one stole a choice morsel. We left them lying in the shade like a lot of contented pussy cats.

We decided to hunt in the afternoon for impala but as we passed our lion pasture of the morning there were our fourteen looking hungrily at us. We could not resist the appeal so we shot them a wildebeest and dragged it down to them. They hardly waited for us to cut it loose before they started out of the bush and before the car had moved off forty yards, they were on it. They were so busy eating they refused to look up to be photographed and we whistled at them, shouted, and blew the horn.

None of it had much effect until I sang to them, "There's a rainbow round my shoulders," and then they all looked up and snarled. We ran off another 200 feet of film and left them, returning to camp as it was too late to hunt further.

We moved camp to the Gurumeti River but had only been on the road an hour before one of the boys saw what he declared to be a big lion. Percival and I climbed out and raced, or at least I hobbled along on my crutches, through an intervening screen of brush to see a cheetah slowly working its way up the hill. It flopped over backwards at my shot and a short chase and three more shots finished it.

We pulled into a very attractive spot at a spring called Kibrori about 11 a.m. and soon camp was settled down as if we had been there a month. Bowen set about collecting birds at once and soon came back with twelve specimens of which he thought a lark might be a new species. In all our camps he has been able to get enough birds in an hour to keep his skinner and himself busy till it was too dark to work.

After tea we drove out on a scouting trip and just as it was getting dark Percival saw a good impala in the brush. I fired and it showed that it was hard hit but we searched half an hour without result. Kimoni insisted that it was lying stone dead not far from us and finally we stumbled on it to find we had killed a twenty-eight inch head. We went back to camp quite happy.

The next morning, three miles from camp down the Gurumeti, we spotted a cow and bull eland feeding along through waist-deep grass. We climbed out of the car and crawled behind a thorn bush as they were feeding in our direction. Things were looking splendid for a good shot when four zebra appeared downwind from us. We knew they would get our wind and probably take the eland off with them in

The men spent an hour watching the wildebeest migration.

their flight. The only question was whether the eland would get within decent shooting range before the zebra caught our scent. I kept the bull covered, determined to shoot no matter what the range, as it had a good head. The eland was about 200 yards away when the zebra snorted and, as it raised its head, I drilled it through the chest. Away it went with the cow and ran hard for a mile and a half when it collapsed. What a job to find the eland in the tall grass but eventually we located it and, as it was still breathing, it was hallaled in proper Mohammedan style. As this was the best meat we could get and there was 1,500 pounds of it, Laura and I drove back to camp for the truck, bringing out a bunch of porters who were immensely pleased at the sight of so much good meat.

This had taken most of the morning so after a short run along the edge of the hills we returned to camp at noon. The afternoon was a washout from the hunting point of view. We met the head of the wildebeest migration coming into the Gurumeti where they eventually break up into small parties and drifted back whence they came, or are slaughtered by the Wandorobo or Ikoma. We sat and watched the migration for an hour - great black lines advancing across the plains. As they drew near it was apparent they were broken up in separate herds, one of which we tried to count and as near as we could come to it, it contained 2,100 head. Each herd was apparently led by an old cow as they plunged along on their slow ceaseless gallop. They ran in a long column six or seven deep and over a mile long. We watched one column turn aside to a small pool for water - the leaders approached it carefully while the herd bunched up. After it was proven safe, there was a mad rush and such crowding as you could hardly conceive. Before more than a few score had quenched their thirst, something frightened them and a mad scramble back through the collected herd followed. Many must be hurt in this attempt to water and thousands are taken by lions and natives as they try to drink.

As the grass had not yet been burned off in the Gurumeti Valley, we decided to look over the Mbalageti River from which direction we had been seeing the smoke of grass fires for the last two days. Our survey of the Gurumeti had proved that the grass was too long to find lion until the natives had burned it off, as they do each year. These two rivers run parallel almost to Lake Victoria and the route we followed between them was about twelve miles.

We found the Mbalageti country thoroughly burned over and the natives already hunting. The first sight that met our eyes as we approached the bank of the river

The zebra in the tree had not been visited.

was a wildebeest, freshly killed by native hunters, with his tail and mane cut off and all the rest left for vultures. The trade in these trophies, one for a fly swatter and the other for a ceremonial headdress, is flourishing, and thousands are sold each year. It appears even a slighter reason than was our sale of buffalo robes for the extermination of these wonderful herds.

We looked over the country for a couple of hours and ran into two lions but they were both unshootable. Our decision was made to move camp to the Mbalageti so we returned to camp. Just a hundred yards from camp our car went out of business. Our engine raced but our wheels stood still. We called the boys and pushed it into camp and then tried to find what was wrong. While I was under the car covered with oil, one of the boys rushed in to announce that a grass fire was only a quarter of a mile away and straight upwind. We all turned and set backfires completely around our camp to protect it and finished our fire line only a few minutes before the main fire reached us. We were safe but it had been anxious work as it would not have been pleasant to have burned up our cars, films and tents.

In the middle of the excitement we heard a violent shooting and turned to see Bowen, through the smoke, bombarding the sky with his shotgun. He explained that swifts came over a fire to catch the insects that it raised and this was his opportunity to collect swifts. He would have collected something if the whole place had burned up.

Finally the fire was out and we still had a camp to move to the Mbalageti, where we arrived just after dark. We went to bed amid a real chorus of lion roars and grunts, which augured well for the next day. On the road over we hit a pig hole with one wheel and bounced Percival off the load. He turned a complete somersault and lit on his face and shoulder. It shook him up badly but no bones were broken.

We really made a good start the next day - up at 4:30 a.m. and away out of camp just before sunup. We followed the direction from which we had heard the grunts the night before and about 9 a.m. came on a kill from which two lions sneaked off as we arrived. We saw two yellow streaks, but had no idea whether they were any good and we did not have a chance to shoot. A little later we saw a cheetah but as I had killed one, we let it go.

As we drove home Laura remarked, "Doesn't that look like a deer's horns in the brush."

The Thomson's gazelle hid among the brush.

We all looked and saw a splendid waterbuck. The waterbuck was much better than the one I had killed so I dropped it. Its horns measured twenty-seven inches in length.

As we arrived at camp we found everybody in a furor. Two lions had been seen entering the donga not 300 yards from camp, so Percival and I piled back in the car and drove over to the donga to see if we could locate them. We stopped the car about ten feet from a clump of brush and just as we pulled up, a lioness stepped out straight in front of us, passed around the bush and disappeared in the donga. We sent the boys in the car upwind to fire the donga while Percival and I sat down to wait. The grass and brush burned fiercely and soon we saw a head pop out and look us over. We could not see enough, however, to judge the lion so let it go back. Eventually, two of them broke cover and trotted away about a hundred yards from us.

It was now apparent that it was an old lion (maneless) and a lioness so we did not shoot. They trotted by us and directly in front of camp so that everybody there had a good view of them. About 4 p.m. we set forth to put out a kill in the hopes of seeing a good lion on it in the morning. About a mile from camp I shot a wildebeest out of a bunch of six at forty yards. It galloped along for seventy-five yards with the others and then turned aside and lay down.

We had started forward when there was a flash of yellow from a clump of scrub not far off and, as the wounded wildebeest jumped to its feet, a lioness landed on its back. The wildebeest staggered forward for perhaps twenty yards when they both went down in a struggling mass of hoofs and tawny paws. At one time the lioness had one of its forelegs over its right shoulder and all the time she was flat on the wildebeest on the upper side as they rolled about. It was over in about a minute but during this time her mate appeared trotting leisurely along in evident certainty she was doing a good job. The lion sat on its haunches ten feet away and watched the finishing touches being put on, and not till all was quiet and the wildebeest had given its last kick did the lion approach nearer. Then, pawing a hind leg out of the way, the lion took its first bite in the belly just in front of the hind leg. The lioness walked around her kill and watched her lord and master get a good start before she settled down to feed. We watched them for a few minutes and then backed away. However, they heard us and moved off the kill a few yards to some slight cover from which they watched our departure.

It was a rare sight. In fact, Percival said he had never seen an actual kill before and he knew of no white man who had. People who have seen a lion kill could testify to it as a streak of yellow, a cloud of dust, and afterwards a dead animal when their approach had driven the lion away. Here we had seen the whole business from start to finish in short grass so there was little if any dust to obstruct our view. We recognized these two lions as the same two we had burned out of the donga in the morning.

These lions had stolen our kill so we went on another mile and shot a zebra, which we dragged under a tree and covered with thorn bushes to keep the birds off till dark. It was a full moon night and as we sat around the campfire that night we heard the lions grunting in all directions. Two were in the donga quite close to camp and before the night was over they had all of us out of bed, as they came within fifty yards of the boys' tent. It was no evening for a nervous woman.

The next morning we started off to visit our kill just as it came light and on the way met the lion and lioness that we had supplied with supper returning from their feast. We were getting tired of seeing these two but let them go. Nothing had visited our kill but hyenas and birds, so we turned up river and traveled the whole morning without seeing another thing. On our return to camp, as might have been expected, the boys announced they had seen a wooly one 200 yards from the campfire.

After lunch we put another zebra kill out, only this time we thought we would be real foxy and hoisted it up to the limb of a tree, with just its head touching the ground. A mile farther downriver we shot two kongoni for another kill and started for camp. On the way we nearly ran over a big lioness that was lying just on the edge of cover. There was quite a scramble in the car till we were sure the lioness was not coming. The lion chorus that night around our campfire was bigger and better than ever. We hung a lantern outside our tent.

At daylight we started for our kills full of bright hopes. The zebra in the tree had not been visited and at the two kongoni we had been running a cafeteria for a lion, lioness and a cub, but they had all departed by the time we arrived. The rest of the morning was a fruitless search. The afternoon proved more interesting, for just before we reached our treed zebra kill, we saw a lioness ambling along. We stopped, as it was headed toward our kill, and gave the lioness ten minutes to settle down to it. We wanted to see how the lioness would handle a kill hung up in this way.

As we moved up slowly the lioness was walking around it as if uncertain how to start. We stopped a hundred yards away and watched it through the glasses. After looking it all over the lioness moved around to the back of the tree where the rope holding up the zebra was tied. The long end of the rope, which we had not used, was coiled up and put up in the crotch of the tree. Deliberately, the lioness rose on its hind legs and caught this coil of rope in its teeth, mouthed it for a moment, and then pulled it down to the ground. Then it tackled the knot where the line to the zebra was made fast. The lioness pulled at this a couple of times and then, getting down, went around to see if its work had had any effect on the kill. It had not, so the lioness walked away in disgust.

Percival said, "Well, I'm beat. The damn lions even try to untie knots. Let's move to some other country."

The next day began at 12:05 a.m. The lions had given us a grand chorus all evening up to the time we turned in. Something woke me at midnight and I decided to get up and have a smoke. I was just lighting a cigarette when I heard a snarl and growl so close at hand I grabbed my gun and ran outside. All the boys were tumbling out of their tents and there was much talking and pointing, but I could make out nothing to shoot at in the darkness, so I went back to bed and to sleep.

At breakfast they all had a story to tell of how this lion had prowled along their tents and only by the grace of God had one of them at that moment decided to come out of his tent. He met the lion face to face not three feet away and it is hard to tell which was the most scared. He dived into the tent and yelled from beneath the blankets. The lion snarled and bolted.

The tent mate of this fellow was our chauffeur, who was scared to death of lions, so we had him in and asked him what it was all about.

He stood before us looking positively ashen and replied, "Bwana, I almost went away last night." We all burst out laughing at his tragic look.

When we tracked the lion and found he had passed within ten feet of the door of our tent where a lantern was burning and had sat down within three feet of this man's tent, it ceased to be a joke. Percival allowed that some of them had to be thinned out or we would have to move camp. Just before it was really light we drove out of camp to visit a kill we had put down a quarter of a mile away. There was a good big lion on it and it took only a minute to step out of the truck and plaster a 220 grain bullet into the lion's chest as it stood looking at us. The lion rose straight up in the air with a roar and collapsed as it came down. We were all sure we had it but a movement in the grass soon told us the lion was making for the donga. We had only a snap shot at the lion before it covered the forty yards to cover. We did everything we could to get the lion out but it either slipped out or was lying there dead.

While we were at it hammer and tongs with everybody on edge and Laura chattering away about nothing till we nearly shot her, the gun boy spied a lioness looking at us from seventy-five yards away. Only its head was visible above the grass but I put in a shot where I thought its neck was and the lioness did a perfect back flip. The lioness lay dead still about half a minute and then crawled to its feet. We hit it three times more before it reached cover but could not anchor the lioness. The lioness got away.

While we were not shooting for trophies but to put heart in the boys, we were sorry to lose these two. As the morning was young we decided to look for the big one. We had covered a lot of country before 10 a.m. and seen nothing when Kimoni,

Prentiss thought zebras looked like toasted horses.

the gun boy, spotted a lioness in thick thorn bush. In the hopes that the lion might be near we drove in and sure enough, way in deep in the shadow was a big lion.

We all looked the lion over, Percival with the glasses, and we all concluded it was a big lion but with only a little mane, so I fired from sixty yards and with a sob it rolled over. I fired twice more just to be sure the lion would stay down and, as it was evidently anchored, turned to see what the lioness had been doing. The lioness was very busy, tail snapping over its crouched form and it sure looked like we were in for a party, but Percival shouted and Ishmaeli blew the motor horn. This was too much for the lioness and it turned and ran. With the lioness gone, out of the grass popped another lioness we had not previously seen. Then we went in to look at our dead lion. It was a big lioness and Percival was the maddest of the whole crowd. Nobody was pleased except the chauffeur, who "almost went away last night." He was pleased at the death of any member of the lion family.

He remarked, "Now that you have come to your senses and are beginning to shoot lions, we will get plenty of big ones. The devils will quit us."

We had lunch and made a fairly early start in order to put out another kill close to camp. We were determined to get the old tuneful devil that kept us awake at night and had tried to steal Ishmaeli. We shot two kongoni and after staking them down, covered them with thorn brush to keep the birds off till dark. Then we made a wide circle out through the brush country.

It was getting on toward 5 p.m. when Percival and I at the same instant saw the "big wooly one" sitting on its haunches like a dog right out in the open. The lion was a hundred yards from any real cover but we prayed we could anchor it as even that distance is not great if they start traveling. It took quite a while to get off my shot as I wanted to be sure. Finally I fired at 110 yards and the lion growled and rolled over on its back. I put in another as quickly as possible to be sure it was down for good. Percival, Kimoni and I advanced in battle formation but it was not until Kimoni pulled its tail and kicked it that I really believed we had the lion. It was the sixty-eighth lion we had seen.

The lion was a splendid specimen, full maned and oversize. It measured nine feet and two inches from tip to tip and Percival estimated the lion's weight at 450 pounds. With great effort five of us loaded it into the truck and started for camp a mile and a quarter away. Kimoni smiled for the first time on the trip, and Ishmaeli muttered a lot about the "devil having now left us, all would be well."

Wildebeest and zebra often grazed together along the Serengeti Plains.

Our arrival in camp caused a great stir. Everybody cheered and shook Laura's and my hand. I suspect they figured they would each get a shilling, but I feel sure there was also real joy and relief, for our continued failure to find one with a mane was getting on everybody's nerves.

We had a wonderful dinner and drank more than usual. While the gramophone was squeaking out some blithe ditty, we heard a snarl and growl and realized our friends of the past nights were still with us. The growl came from not forty yards off the porters' tents and when we got there the porters were scared to death.

We decided to give them a run for it on the truck, so we all piled in and with lights blazing, set forth on a wild ride around camp. We saw nothing and returned after a few minutes to go to bed.

We slept till 11 p.m. when more grunts prompted the porters to urge another trip in the car. We all piled in - most of us scantily clad - I had hastily pulled on Laura's pink silk dressing gown, and started out on a mad whirl through the trees. Percival and I were standing up, leaning over the cab with our guns, and every jolt pushed the cab halfway through our stomachs. We must have been a sight - my pink gown flapping in the breeze and Percival's raincoat streaming out behind - as we tore along.

We had driven only a short distance before we picked up two lions in the headlights and with a yell of triumph the Kavirondo driver pushed after them. Percival and I began to fire but the chance of hitting within fifty feet of the lions was extremely slim as the truck was bouncing like a wild thing. We ran them together through the bush for half a mile with everybody yelling advice and, if they could think of no advice, just yelling either to encourage us or discourage the lions.

Then they separated and we took after one for another quarter of a mile until we had fired our last cartridge. We turned home, patting ourselves on the back that at least we had run these two lions out of the country.

Not at all - by 2 a.m. they had returned and for the rest of the night kept us all more or less awake. This was the most lionly day I ever hope to experience.

We all came to breakfast yawning visibly. The boys had slept little if any and the opinion was unanimous that these two lions in particular had an unpleasant interest in our persons. We decided to retreat and let them have the field of battle, so after a short run around to visit the two kills we had out, where we saw only a lioness, we packed the trucks and started back to the Seronera River.

A leisurely time in camp.

The day was overcast and showery, so while we made a short camera hunting trip in the afternoon, we gave it up for a leisurely time in camp. The strain of peering under every bush for a good lion was over and we could now relax. We had kept our "fly on the water" every morning and evening for twenty-one days and with the fish now in the creel, we could rest.

We had a hard rain during the night but it broke clear in the morning with all the dust washed out of the air. It looked right for photographs so we fared forth with all the film magazines loaded. The plain's game for some reason was wild and we could not even get near enough to the zebra to get anything but group pictures.

Late in the afternoon we succeeded in getting some long-range pictures of impala and after it was too dark to photograph, the zebra stood about in herds right near the car.

We turned the day into a small buck shooting day by killing a couple of dik-dik the smallest of the antelope family, to match my eland, which is the largest. Also, we shot a steinbok almost as small and a pair of klipspringers. These later gave us a lot of fun as they bounced about among the rocks of a kopi. They always appeared where you did not expect them and disappeared before you could get the gun on them. There was the cheerful feeling you could kick out a leopard as you prowled about among the rocks.

On June 29th we started for Nairobi and then, after a run of seventy-five miles, camped at Sandy River where, for the first time in two weeks, we were out of the tsetse fly belt. We were glad of it as they had chewed our neck and ankles till they were raw. Laura traveled with a flit gun till we were sore with laughing at her. She always insisted in using it just when we were skirting a dense cover and all keyed up that a lion was going to bounce out at us.

By July 1st we reached Nairobi and my first job was to have an x-ray taken of my leg. It confirmed the fracture but both bones were knitting in place. The old doctor had a whole lot of bright conversation about how lucky I was and how only by the grace of God I was able to keep it in place so it could knit. However, it did knit and that's that.

As I sat in the doctor's office each day for electrical treatment to make it knit faster, I became acquainted with Jack Lucy, a white hunter who was having his arm massaged after a lion mauling. Lucy had been out with some Italians on safari the previous February and in the first few days out they put up a lion that took cover in a donga. Lucy went round to drive it to the hunters and practically stepped on the lion at the edge of cover. It jumped on him and as the lion went down he shot it through the mouth. Lucy was clawed on the shoulder and back and as he lay perfectly still the lion only tore two mouthfuls out of his left arm and then lay alongside him watching the approach of Dick Pedler who was running in answer to Lucy's cry for help. Pedler came in sight of Lucy but could not see the lion that was laying behind him. Lucy did not dare move but signaled with his eyes where the lion was, and Pedler killed it just as it rose up to charge him or further worry Lucy. Pedler then ran to the car for morphine and pomangenate and had only gone a few yards when he put up a lioness. The lioness charged but he shot straight enough to literally kill it in mid-air. Pedler then and there quit lion hunting.

Lucy was brought in more dead than alive and after five months just was getting back slightly the use of his arm. After all this, the Italians claimed and took the lion skin.

After some of the Continental sportsmen, Americans probably enjoy the worst reputation here and, as near as I can make out, this is largely due to Stewart Edward

Masai women

White, who is reported to have killed sixty-five lions on one trip. It may be said that at that time there was no limit to the bag of lions allowed by law, but that is no justification for anyone shooting all the lions he sees. We could have killed fifty or sixty out of the seventy-one we saw, but I am sorry we killed more than one. An American named Grant from New York killed twenty-six lions and left nine wounded. Another American had sixteen cheetah skins lying in Nairobi, which he killed despite the limit of two allowed by law. The license allows you to kill 266 animals, plus leopard, hyena and jackal, which are classed as vermin. That ought to be more than plenty.

By July 7th I was getting worried about the trucks that we had left with Percival and his wife in Tanganyika. However, they finally appeared with a terrible story of rain and mud. They had encountered a terrific storm, which deeply filled the river's bank, turned the black cotton soil into a sticky ooze, and left three inches of hail on the ground. All this in July in Central Africa where you are supposed to be hot. They had a hard time keeping the boys from freezing to death. All the trucks were behind them struggling through the mud and as there was no immediate prospect of their arriving for at least another day, I went down with them to Machakos to their farm for the night. I wanted to see a bit of African farm life. After three years drought and two years locusts, I saw plenty and it was sad.

Just as we were leaving for Nairobi a boy rushed in to tell us that the locusts had arrived in the only remaining wheat field. It was a terrible blow as it meant practically ruin and we all tore out there with all the boys available. By some act of providence, the swarm had settled for only a few minutes and passed on.

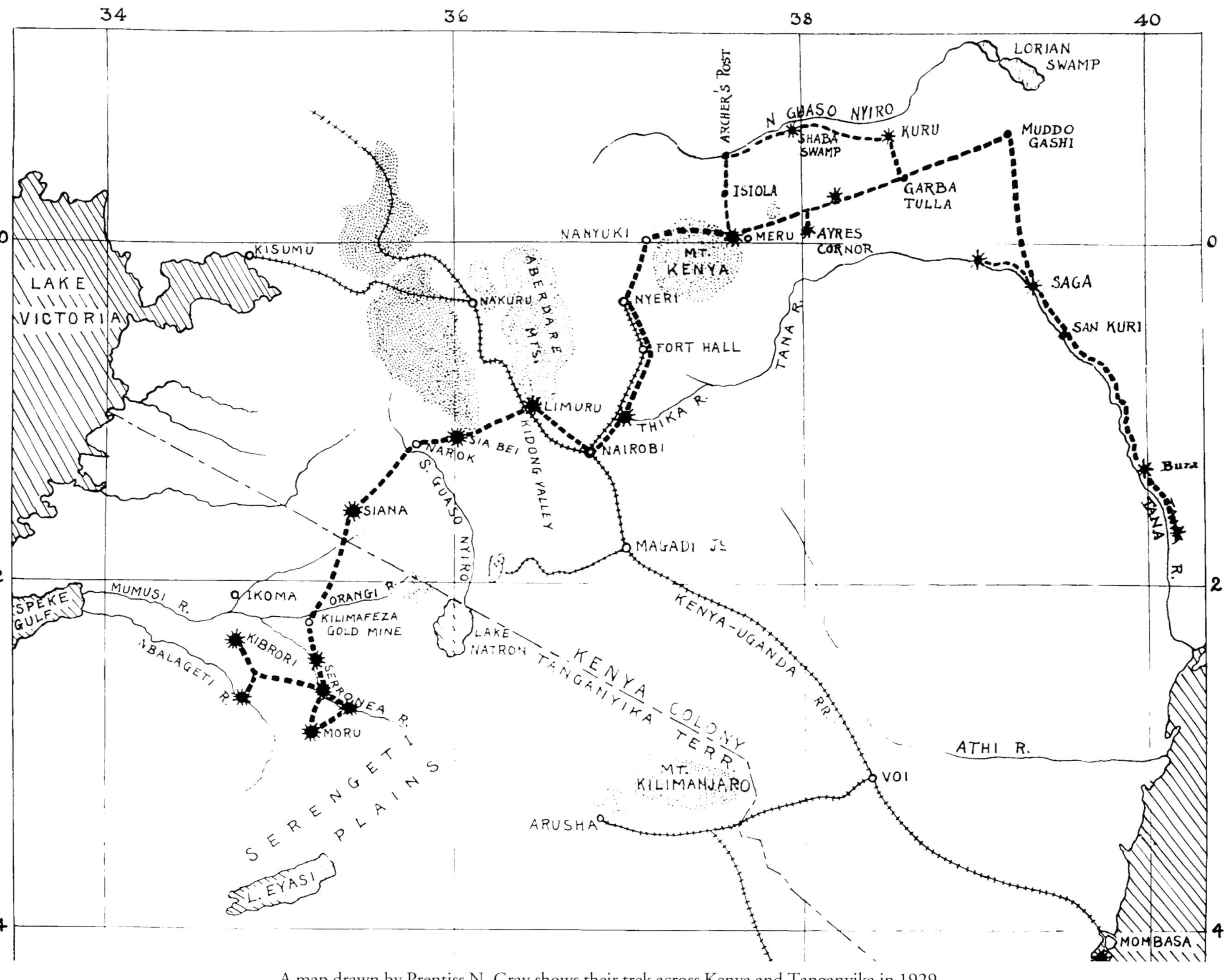

A map drawn by Prentiss N. Gray shows their trek across Kenya and Tanganyika in 1929. The stars drawn on the map indicate locations of specimen collection.

KENYA

PART THREE

DESERT GAME AND WATER HOLES

IT was not until July 12th that we saw the last of Nairobi. We were headed north for elephant, rhino, Cape buffalo, and pictures at the desert water holes. We had in mind to gather groups of gerenuk and Hunter's antelope to complete our bag for the Philadelphia Academy.

We stopped for a late lunch at Thika, where the hotel stands between two wonderful waterfalls. We drove on past Fort Hall to Nyeri, where we arrived at 8:30 p.m. at the White Rhino Hotel after doing a flat hundred miles.

We had a run of eighty-six miles ahead of us to Meru. The track, for it could not be called a road, led through Nanyuki, which is on the Equator - the line passing just through the bridge on the edge of town. There we photographed the trucks while I stood about in an eider-down coat and shivered, for the elevation was 6,700 feet and it was cold.

During the afternoon we rose to 8,300 feet on the slopes of Kenya, where for miles we traveled across open plains in the face of a wind that cut like a knife. Then we entered the forest and dropped down to 6,100 feet at Pat Ayres' sawmill at Meru. Here we made a very attractive camp for Bowen, whom we proposed to leave for a month while we descended still farther to the Tana River.

We made rather a late start the next day out of Meru, as the stores had to be divided to provision Bowen for this month. However, we were on the road by 11 a.m. and, with our two trucks, moved down the road twenty-five miles to Isiola, where we stopped for a chat and a glass of beer with District Commissioner Hemstead. We saw our first game since leaving Nairobi nearly 200 miles behind, in

The motor safari began the trip.

this stretch. First ostriches, then a few Grant's gazelle of a type different from the Robert's gazelle, which we had seen in Tanganyika. These were smaller and their horns went straight up with very little spread. Then I caught my first glimpse of oryx and was surprised, although I had seen many in pictures, at the graceful length of their slender horns and their striking coloration. Then gerenuk appeared with their long necks and slender bodies and I felt quite cheered up as I wanted a group of these for the Museum in case we failed on the giant sable.

We passed Rattray's zebra farm. The government, in order to foster this attempt to domesticate the Grevy's zebra, had stopped all shooting of these beasts south of the Uaso Nyiro, and Rattray was permitted to conduct drives periodically, setting out long wings and drifting the zebra for miles into these wings that lead to his catching boma. It then took him about three months to get them tame enough to handle, whereupon he sold them for £150 each.

He only had six in his boma when we were there and I was unable to learn of anyone in Africa who had paid £150 for one to use as a draft animal, although some had been sold abroad. A good big ox costs only £6 and a mule £15, so unless he can establish the fact these zebra will breed in captivity, it is difficult to see that he is benefiting the country to any extent. If it were possible to domesticate the zebra as a draft animal and the eland as a meat producer, both being immune to the local diseases, it would solve many problems of this country.

Just before we reached Archer's Post, a new military road (really only a track but any place a car has ever been is called a road in this country) turns off down the Uaso Nyiro to the east. This we took and bumped along over lava for nearly thirty miles. We were now in a desert country of lava and sand - terribly hard pulling for the cars and desperately hard on tires. It was getting hot, too, for our barometer read only 2,700 feet. We made camp for the night on the banks of the Uaso Nyiro, which means white water, but the stream was a very dirty yellow. The ground was too full of stones to drive in the tent pegs so we hung a tarpaulin between two thorn bushes and put our cots under that.

We had selected this site on the river to camp because it was near the Shaba Swamp where we hoped to get some water hole pictures. We finally located the swamp but found a great deal too much water and consequently too many places for the animals to drink. However, we decided to give it a try and chose a place at the eastern end of the swamp where the game trails looked particularly well worn.

Thika Falls

Here we built a blind such as has never been seen before. There was no green stuff about except on the top of the trees and, therefore, we had to build it of old logs and dried thorn limbs. We put in a background of canvas and a top fly of americani dipped in motor oil and rubbed in the dirt. We thought the animals would see it in a minute but it was hardly complete before a herd of thirty-six oryx walked straight up to the water and let me take 200 feet of film and a dozen stills. During the morning, a few Grant's gazelle came in but they seemed to be more fearful of our blind than the oryx. Shortly after noon another herd of oryx accompanied by some Grant's gazelle came in and I gathered quite a lot of photographs of them.

For two hours the zebra had been standing off a couple of hundred yards among the thorn bushes watching us, trying to make up their minds that all was as it should be. Finally, six of them came down among the trees behind us and we turned the cameras about and got some footage. By 5 p.m. it had clouded up heavily so we gave it up for the day and went off to kill some meat for the men. I missed a Grant's gazelle and Percival, after much shooting, shot one in the hind leg. Then followed a long chase of a couple of miles across lava, which put quite a strain on my bad foot. We never did get the Grant's gazelle and returned to camp after dark very mad.

We were up at 4:30 a.m. to change films and were settled in our blind before 7:30 a.m. It was, however, not until 9:30 a.m. that the first game came in and then a few Grant's gazelle straggled along. We soon found the wind had shifted and these animals did not care for our scent as they snorted much like whitetail deer and stamped their forefeet. We had to work very slowly behind our scanty blind and the result was few pictures and not very good ones.

About 10:30 a.m. a herd of about forty oryx appeared and I began taking film furiously. They paid no attention to us and were so busy racing about in play they did not hear the cameras running. Two bulls staged a grand fight and pushed each other all over the open space with a great clashing of horns.

Finally, emboldened by the presence of the oryx, five Grant's gazelle came in with much snorting. They, however, liked our scent less the nearer they approached the water and just as they reached it they whirled and fled, taking most of the oryx with them. The rest only stayed a short time before they departed to join the herd.

A big herd of Grevy's zebra appeared about noon but they drank above us and

"A few Grant's gazelle came in but they seemed to be more fearful of our blind than the oryx."

Even a conspicuous blind did not keep the game from water. Here stands the blind at Shaba Swamp.

Zebra herds were abundant.

A large herd of oryx appeared and Prent began taking film furiously.

stood about in the dense shade behind us for an hour. They kept us on the "qui vive" but never gave us a chance for a photograph.

We had a few casual visitors during the afternoon but the wind continued in the wrong quarter and the Grant's gazelle went on snorting and stamping and scaring everything else. We tried hanging a ground sheet behind our thorn screen to cover up all motion of working with cameras, and this helped a little but the game was so terrified that we could expect but little to come in. Therefore, at 4 p.m. we went back to camp.

During the night the flashlight camera went off with a bang that woke the whole camp at 12:45 a.m. Just before we went to bed a rhino had snorted quite close to camp and I thought it was upon us and Percival was shooting at it. I bounced out of bed and grabbed a gun but all seemed to be quiet and then it dawned on me it was the flashlight camera.

As daylight came we went out to the flash camera and found some jackals near it. The camera had been exposed by them to our disgust as we wanted nothing less than a rhino. I fired a whole volley of shots at these pests without doing them any great damage.

Percival and I were in the blind by 7 a.m. but did not expect anything to appear until about 10 a.m. However, a solitary Grant's gazelle and oryx and finally five common zebra came within range and we had quite a lot of film exposed before we expected the day's fun to start. Things rather dragged just when we thought should be the time the game should drink. It is ever thus with wild animals. They always act just as Fred Feutz used to say of the elk in Wyoming, "These damn elk ain't got no principles." We had, however, very fair luck with small groups of zebra and oryx and a single Grant's gazelle until it approached the time for the trucks to pick us up, for we were moving camp forty miles farther east to another water hole.

Just before they arrived I saw a thumping big oryx, which Percival assured me had a good head. So we left the blind and started a stalk as it was about 300 yards off. At 150 yards I shot and oryx came down. Its head measured 31 1/4 inches and did me very well.

Just then two Boran natives, who live in this desert country, appeared from nowhere so we gave them the meat as our Mohammedans would not have it. They were so pleased to find all this food without having to hunt it themselves they promptly asked us for matches and tobacco, too. We took the head and Hamisi the

Grant's gazelles came in with great snorting.

One oryx to the right stands guard.

skinner was overjoyed at the prospect of something to do after his long idleness.

We drove slowly the rest of the afternoon as the road was across lava beds that badly cut the tires. Just before we made camp we saw two gerenuk and I shot the male as the first of the group for the museum. I shot two solids through the gerenuk well forward so as not to damage the hide but it ran a full 200 yards. I came to the conclusion it was better to use soft-nosed bullets. They kill quicker and one can always sew up the skin.

We made camp at a most attractive water hole called Kuru, seventy-five miles east of Archer's Post. Here we proposed to stay a few days collecting the gerenuk group and photographing while one of the cars returned to Meru for petrol to take us 255 miles to the elephant country and back.

Our first job was to build a blind and we found a splendid location with plenty of palm trees near at hand with which to construct it. After an hour's work, we turned out what we considered a work of art in blinds and sending the boys back to camp Percival and I sat down to wait for our subjects. They were, however, in no hurry to come along and after four hours we had not seen a living thing except a few doves. We were about to give it up as a bad job as noon had passed, when suddenly appeared a bunch of five gerenuk.

I thought of the four years Martin Johnson had worked to get his first picture of gerenuk. It flashed into my mind the interest these pictures would have to the museum in connection with the group of gerenuk we were collecting. Then the cameras began to work and before the animals moved off they had performed all their tricks and we had 600 feet of film.

The gerenuk is a small buck weighing about sixty pounds live weight. It has a deep rufous faun coat with a broad brown stripe down the back. The extraordinary thing about it is his long neck. It is almost as long in proportion to his body as a giraffe. The gerenuk uses it to good advantage as the animal is a browser and when it cannot reach the green top of thorn bushes within four feet from the ground, the gerenuk rises on its hind legs, hooks its front feet into the branches above it, or plants one of them against the trunk of the bush, and goes to work eating off the top. The gerenuk stands absolutely straight up so that its neck, body and hind legs make a straight vertical line. It was a rare chance to get this bunch of five for so long a time before us, although they were seventy-five yards away.

We set the flash camera on our return to camp and before we finished dinner it

Their first job near the water hole at Kuru was to construct a blind. After an hour's work, Prent and Percival turned out what they considered a "work of art."

A Grant's gazelle watches the cameraman.

went off with a bang, whereupon the boys in camp let out a yell. They liked this camera outfit because it made a noise and scared the animal. They seemed to get enjoyment out of thinking of the beast's surprise. They did not understand what the movies or the stills were all about, although Percival overheard the skinner tell one of the other men one morning while we were building a blind.

"This taking pictures is just play but they must do it to show the memsahib, who has gone back to America, that they have been busy and not up to mischief," he said.

I decided to put aside the cameras the next morning and get ahead with the gerenuk group. In this hot country the skinner can handle only one animal at a time so we could not kill more than one beast per day for him to work on, even if we had the chance. If left only a few hours after killing, the skin is liable to slip. We had not gone 200 yards from camp before I saw a gerenuk doe and dropped her. We had the skinner taking off the skin within ten minutes and as the day was young, I went back to my camera work in the blind. We had not been there very long before the same bunch of gerenuk appeared but they did not behave as well as the previous day, feeding farther away and spending most of their time behind bushes. They had not the slightest idea we were about so it was not due to fear, but they just found better food some place else instead of in front of our cameras. They had fed off by noon so that about 1 p.m. we went back to camp for lunch.

We decided to set the flash for rhino with a trip wire on a game trail. I returned to the blind early in the afternoon and was only comfortably settled when the flash exploded. It was over a mile away but some waterbuck that were just coming into the water hole turn tail and fled. We waited patiently for their return and in half an hour they appeared bringing with them a Grevy's zebra, which I particularly wanted to photograph. For an hour I had a riot of pictures. Two more Grevy's strolled in and the waterbuck behaved beautifully. At last the final exposure was made as we had run out of film, having taken 1,000 feet and four dozen stills.

Then we returned to camp just as it was getting dark and remembered that the flash camera needed resetting. Neither Percival nor I cared for the half-mile walk upriver in the dark as we suspected some foolish rhino might not like our visit, but with heavy guns in hand and more guns with the gun bearers, we started and finished without trouble.

It was a gorgeous African night - almost full moon - and for several hours after

The waterbuck behaved beautifully as Prent photographed them.

dinner we sat in front of the tents and drank in its beauty. Strange noises were all about us. A rhino snorted, a jackal yapped, and finally, far off, a lion began to grunt.

Percival awoke next morning with a fever so I insisted he stay in bed. I started out early for our daily gerenuk hunt but did not see any until we had traveled over an hour. Then Kimoni took me on an exciting stalk that ended a hundred yards from a good buck. The buck dropped in its tracks at the shot and we started back to camp.

At 9:30 a.m. we were in the blind again and although I waxed exceeding hungry by 1 p.m., we were so busy from 9:30 a.m. until 3 p.m. that I did not have time to sit down. There was a constant procession of Grant's gazelle, waterbucks, and gerenuk. The Grant's and waterbuck came so close to the blind I thought they were going to eat it. I exposed every foot of film I had and wished for more. Finally, we had to walk out of the blind with waterbuck scattered all over the landscape in front of us. Their surprise at the sight of us emerging from a palm tree was wonderful to behold.

Percival was a few days getting his fever down with thirty grains of quinine a day, but finally we were on the road again. After twenty miles we came to Garba Tulla, which sounds like a town but really is only a collection of wattle-and-dab native huts and an Indian trader's corrugated iron store. Here we learned the water had given out at Muddo Gashi where we had intended to camp and we decided to run on only ten miles to the last water before we started on the long waterless hop of 140 miles to San Kuri on the Tana River. Here we camped and put Percival back to bed. My gun bearer, Kimoni, and Percival's boy, Katy, were also down with fever, so I got real excited and took five grains of quinine myself when I heard a mosquito buzz.

I tried for a gerenuk in the afternoon but shot badly and missed two. It's no excuse, but these wary beasts always seem to hide behind a bush with their head just over the top. Then you have to guess where the body is and as it is only ten inches wide if they stand facing you, it is not much of a target. I returned to camp thoroughly disgusted.

We told the boys to call us early for the long hop and they surely did it. At 3:30 a.m., I was pulled out of bed with the camp going down all about me.

We had to dig holes in a sand river to get enough water to fill all the petrol tins

A Grant's gazelle grazes.

we wanted to carry, but we finally ladled out enough from these pits and started. After forty-four miles we ran into Muddo Gashi and found only a few people getting the necessary water on which to live, which was not much, out of a deep hole in the sand river. The country was dry as a bone and monotonous to the last degree. The land was flat as far as you could see without a suspicion of mountains or hills in any direction, covered with a low thorn bush that provided no shade to the ground beneath. Yet here and there was game - gerenuk, giraffe and dik-dik - and we wondered how they existed so far from water. We spotted a cheetah on top of an ant hill and I missed a wonderful shot at seventy-five yards. This seemed to be my off time again and I hoped it would be over before we got to elephant as it would be serious to miss them.

Finally, we began to drop down a gradual slope to the Tana River. It lay before us in a thin line of green trees and to our hot eyes, looked wonderful. We reached the river at Saga, a native village of five huts, but twenty-three miles above San Kuri where we had planned to camp. However, we off loaded right there, thankful that water was at hand and that the fever patients had come through so well.

It was full moon and after Percival had been put to bed I sat out in front of the tent and dreamed. A soft cheerful hum came from the boys' tents. Some music of sorts from a pipe could be heard from the Boran huts. The same moon a few hours later would be shining on my family in Jackson Hole, Wyoming.

We started our last jump toward the coast early the next morning and after twenty-three miles came to the burned ruins of San Kuri. The road was very bad but by 1 p.m. we had covered another seventy miles and stopped at Bura, where we had tea with District Commissioner Captain Mahoney. We gathered all the elephant dope of which he was possessed and at 4 p.m. started again for the camp where we expected to find Hunter's antelope.

After a run of thirty-five miles we saw our first Hunter's antelope, a bunch of about twenty, and I dropped a good bull at 230 yards. His horns measured 23 1/2 inches on the front curve. We had just time to skin it out before total darkness. Percival, I believe, was more thrilled that I over this beast. It was the first one he had ever seen, as, in fact, only a few have been killed. The horns looked much more like those of an impala than those of a hartebeest, to which family it belonged. The body, however, was typical with the high withers sloping sharply down to the hind quarters. A long white tail looked strangely out of place even against the very light

Garba Tulla was a collection of native huts and an Indian trader's corrugated iron store.

"After forty-four miles we ran into Muddo Gashi and found only a few people getting water."

A Hunter's antelope was dropped at 230 yards. Few specimens had ever been collected, so Prent was delighted to collect one for The Academy of Natural Sciences of Philadelphia.

Nomadic Borans passed the expedition's camp.

cream-colored coat of the animal. Although these animals have been hunted very little, they were extremely wary and we found it impossible in the few days of our stay to approach any of them nearer than 175 yards.

DeWatteville is the only person to collect a group for any museum and there is no specimen in any museum in America. That was why we had come.

We were only 100 feet above sea level and eighty miles from the coast in an absolutely waterless desert about forty miles south of the Equator, and yet I wore my eider-down coat during dinner and slept under a blanket. During the night our waterless desert turned on a pouring rainstorm and we were nearly drowned out. However, we continued our hunt for Hunter's antelope and Percival knocked over a splendid buck. It measured on the front curve 26 inches. We had just finished skinning out the head when another deluge came and we beat it for camp.

In the afternoon we hunted about five miles west. There I found a group of Hunter's antelope and killed a cow. We took the measurements and rushed it back to camp in an endeavor to save the skin. It was dark when we arrived but the skinner went straight to work and we heard him singing over his job far into the night. It was quite a task in this hot climate to get a skin off before the hair slips, especially as we could only make one cut in the museum skins and the carcass has to come out in pieces through this cut.

It poured hard all night and the desert looked like a lake in the morning. The road was sodden. We wanted one more Hunter's antelope and after an hour's search we found four bulls, which made off before we could get a shot. We took up the trail and for two hours followed their every twist and turn as they fed along. They were ignorant that we were following but gave us only glimpses of them as they moved through the brush 200 and 300 yards away. We could thank the rain for softening the ground so we could see the spoor to track easily and fast but that is all we could thank it for. It was slippery and wet and cold and damn disagreeable.

At last Kimoni motioned me forward and I had a shot at 175 yards. I missed the first, scored with the second, and took the buck off his feet with the third. The head was a shade better than my first and measured:

On the front curve	25-1/8 inches
Straight	21-1/4 inches
Circumference	8-3/8 inches
Spread	11 inches

Bowen was left at Meru for a month while Prentiss and Percival made their way to the Tana River.

The men stopped at a native village on the banks of the Tana River.

We now had all the specimens that the law allowed us and we headed our cars back to Bura. After sticking in every mud hole, we moved the trucks four miles in the first hour. The second hour we did five miles and then the soil changed and we made about eight miles an hour to Bura, where we arrived just before dark. The district commissioner greeted us effusively and soon we were settled in his boma and enjoying a hot bath and dry clothes. He told us that in his opinion, the Hunter's antelope occupied a belt about thirty-five or forty miles wide, stretching from the Tana River north to Lak Dera in Jubaland, about 160 miles. Nowhere else in the world were they found.

We waited for the road to dry a bit in the morning, for even here they had had two inches of rain. At 10 a.m. we were off and after we had traveled twenty miles we ran out of any sign of rain and from there to Saga, a total distance of ninety-four miles, we ran before 6 p.m., although we stopped on the road to shoot a Grant's gazelle for meat and a young gerenuk bull for the museum group. From here on we were to think nothing but elephants.

We wasted an entire day just sitting. Kimoni and the local guides were busy trying to recruit porters, camels or canoes to take our loads upriver to the point where we were to start hunting. Every Boran who owned a camel was just starting on a trip or the camel was lame. Every prospective porter had some maize to harvest and all the canoes were upriver or someplace else. They thought it would make a better bargain if we needed them badly.

Finally, Percival announced we would start in the morning with our own porters, going as light as necessary to do this. At once two canoes were produced and plenty of porters. We loaded the dugouts, which looked as if they were going to twist over before anything was put in them, and with ten porters also carrying loads, started upstream. We walked until noon, fording several knee-deep estuaries, until the guide called a halt as he declared the canoes could pole upstream no farther in the day.

We were off again by daylight and after two hours walking came to a village of six or seven grass huts. Here we paused to ask the latest news of "Tembo." The guides were gone a couple of hours visiting the shambas and finally came back with news that a herd of elephants had come down to the river the previous night but their tracks led straight back into the desert.

While we were listening to this report, the chief of these parts arrived out of

Philip Percival talks to a native chief.

breath. He was attired in a pink undershirt and a black umbrella and had come on the run two miles from his village to be sure the white men did not get away till they had seen his raiment. He persuaded us to pitch our camp at his village and promised to have his men scour the country for tracks each day till we killed. When this was arranged, he produced a lame man who had severed the tendons just above the heel and demanded we cure him. The still open wound was a running sore and his leg was swollen to the knee. There was nothing we could do except arrange for a canoe to take him to the hospital at Bura, ninety miles away, but I did tie up his foot with a nice white bandage and a pad of Vick's salve. I don't believe it helped much but it gave him a certain distinction in the village, which he seemed to enjoy.

Before daylight we started into the bush. We soon passed out of the cultivated area, which did not extend more than a quarter of a mile back from the river. Then we passed a strip of rank elephant grass interspersed with tall trees and prickly thorn bushes and open glades beautiful to look upon but devilish to travel. The glades contained a low thorny vine that stuck your ankles and entangled your feet. After a quarter of a mile of this terrain we were out in the desert with its covering of thorn bushes of every description.

We made a cast of about six miles parallel to the river, looking for tracks of elephants returning from their nocturnal drink. We were only able to find the tracks of one small herd of cows made the previous day so we damned the whole area and, returning to camp, ordered a move ten miles farther upstream to a point where one of our scouts had reported more sign of elephant.

On the way we passed through one sizable village where they were holding a funeral and such a din of drums and yells you never heard. Here we crossed the river in a dugout, which upset on its third trip with six men in it. Percival and I were safely sitting on the farther bank but there were a few nervous moments before we counted all six men crawling out on the bank. Luckily the crocs did not get a one.

One of our scouts reported finding the tracks of three good bull elephants so we started, while it was still dark. Before 7 a.m. the scout had picked up the tracks, one of which was a good big track measuring twenty three inches in diameter. We were off like hounds, walking fast through the desert scrub although the wait a bit thorns made us sometimes tarry and marked the arms and legs of the black men with white lines. About 10 a.m. our bulls joined a herd of cows and they all carried

Boran women carry jugs of water.

on together for a while. We realized we were getting close as we came on hot dung and the sap was still oozing out of broken branches on which they had fed.

Suddenly, there was a shift in the wind and the light breeze began to blow from our backs directly along the direction of the tracks. We knew the game was up and 100 yards farther the tracks showed where the whole herd had shuffled off in haste and our three bulls had gone off by themselves. We had been five hours on the track but there was nothing to do but return to camp.

We crossed the river the next day to hunt the south bank of the Tana. We traveled upstream for an hour looking for tracks and found them leading from the river bank back into thick bush. The tangle was impenetrable except where the elephants had broken their way through it. The thorn trees and scrub met twenty feet over our heads and we crawled through, bent double or on hands and knees. I did not care for this wiggling my way down a tunnel with solid walls of thorns on both sides and overhead and a tangle of loose branches underneath to catch an unwary footstep. I concluded if this was the proper way to hunt elephants I'd have to stick it, but for the life of me I could not imagine how I was to see the elephant before I opened fire. Ten feet was the extreme limit of our vision except straight down the tunnel ahead or behind and as it was a very twisty path we could often hardly see so far in any direction.

We crept along in single file for an hour when a crashing of branches and vague grunts and squeals told us the herd was feeding not far ahead. Percival and I took our guns from the bearers and moved up toward the head of the line directly behind the guide. So we traveled for another quarter of a mile with the noise of the feeding elephants gradually getting louder. The brush was getting no thinner. Suddenly, there was a crash almost alongside us and we saw the wall of thorns on our left sway. That was enough - the whole bunch broke and tore precipitately back down the tunnel. Each man sought a niche off the trail and dived into the side walls wiggling as far away from the trail as possible.

The noise of the herd died down and nothing more happened. At the end of five minutes, which seemed an age, one by one we crawled back into the trail, each looking scared and shamefaced. We held a whispered conference and most of us, including Percival and old Kimoni, pointed out in the past they had lost no elephants in this kind of bush. However, the guide assured us the bush would soon open up, giving us a chance to see something, and so we crept on.

First, we sought out the spot where the elephant had been that gave us the fright and found it not ten yards off our trail. The main herd had been feeding twenty to thirty yards from us when they took fright. For some reason, it all seemed indescribably funny and we each described in whispers what the other had done during the rout. Several barked shins were manifest, and we concluded that a smoke and a chance to dig thorns out of our legs and hands were the next order of the day. Meanwhile, we hoped the herd would settle down again and this time in some more open place. After half an hour, we started on once more and soon heard the elephants noisily feeding not far ahead. The bush, too, was getting somewhat better and in places we could see twenty or thirty yards.

Our hopes were getting into about the fourth heaven when an ungodly crash

The elephant camp

broke just behind us. The first was followed by a positive roar as another herd, that we had passed without knowing they were there, caught our wind and went crazy. This stirred up the herd we were following and the forest positively rained elephants.

There was no argument in anybody's mind this time what to do. It was run like hell some place. Every place I tried to go seemed directly toward more crashing so finally I just dove into the thorns and crawled as far off any path as I could get. Gradually, the roar died down again and the boys began to appear in the trail. We held a council of war and decided we had had enough and were going back to camp. A double-barreled cordite rifle was as useless in this kind of stuff as a pea

A couple watches the men pass.

Views of a native village in elephant country

shooter, because you could see nothing at which to shoot before you were hit. Seven tons of elephant treading on one's stomach is not an attractive demise. We reached camp before noon and I read Ibsen's *Doll's House* and *Ghosts* to try to calm my soul and cheer me up.

We decided to stay on the more open northern bank of the river and started our next hunt an hour before daylight. We picked our way through the thick bush that extended back from the river bank a quarter of a mile, and came out into the desert. Here it was easier traveling as we could avoid the thorn trees even in the dim light. We had been traveling about half an hour when we heard a crash as an elephant ripped a limb from a tree. More noise of breaking branches told us we were close to a herd feeding as it moved back from the river. We maneuvered for a position downwind from them and traveled along parallel to their course till it was light enough for us to see their ivory as well as our sights.

Then we left the local guides and the porters and Percival and I, with our gunbearers, started to close in. Through the thorns we could make out shadowy shapes. We moved cautiously up to about eighty yards in a rather open place through which we expected the elephants to pass. Suddenly, an old cow stepped out and faced us. In my ignorance I did not know the elephant cow could not see so far and I was sure it was coming but it was just by chance that the cow stood and looked in our direction. After a moment the cow passed on and was followed by seven more in single file.

They looked just as they do in the circus and I remember thinking, "I wonder if they will catch hold of each other's tails."

Percival and the gun bearers were looking at nothing but the ivory and it was a sad blow when they announced there was nothing shootable in the herd. To me, the ivory on two bulls looked enormous but I was told that while it was long it was too slender.

It was a good start, however, for the day and, we hoped, augured well for the rest of it. However, we spent the next four hours tramping the bush without cutting a single track. This was disheartening and we were all very hot and tired when we struck the track of a solitary bull going toward the river. It had been made the previous night but it was a long tramp to follow it to the river and back again. We cast about for the bull's return track and a quarter of a mile farther east we struck it. We were all on edge again at once and although the wind was bad for the course it

The ivory tusks were cut from the bull elephant with an axe. Porters carried them to camp.

apparently had laid, we started after the bull. Within half a mile we heard a twig snap and knew we were up with it. As hurriedly as possible we ran for a position downwind and reaching a point where the ashes shaken from a little sack drifted on the wind away from the bull's position, we started to close in.

Soon we made out the elephant's shape through the brush but I could not believe it could tower so high above us nor bulk so large. We could see no ivory, however, and Percival kept moving closer, making no attempt to keep under cover but watching the gun bearer shake fine ashes from the bag. As long as the wind was right Percival had no fear of alarming the elephant. We were within about twenty yards before we could make out that the bull was resting its tusks in a thorn tree, and finally got a good look at both of them.

Then Percival whispered to me, "Take him."

The fear came into my mind that if I shot through this tangle of brush my bullet might be diverted by a small branch. I maneuvered for a clear space and it seemed an age before I could see the bull elephant's shoulder clearly without intervening scrub. Then I let go with one barrel, followed by the second as soon as I could get my sights back on him.

I thought that ought to do the job but Percival yelled, "Keep on shooting as long as he is up." Kimoni pushed fresh shells into my hand.

The elephant had, meanwhile, wheeled with a prodigious snort and was crashing through the bush. I fired four times more and, wondering why it did not come down, looked about for a tree to get behind in case the bull turned rusty. There was nothing in sight except little things the bull could have been pulled up by the roots to beat us with. Then the bull came into a clear space and seemed to hesitate. I put two more shots into it and the bull sagged at the rear and went down with a terrific crash. Never was a sound more welcome than this crash. The elephant dropped just thirty yards from where it had stood and my first shots had been fired at a distance of twenty-two yards.

As we approached I thought we had shot a single tusker, as one tooth was completely buried in the sand. The bull bulked big and as we measured it, the bull seemed to grow larger. The tape showed it stood ten feet ten inches high at the shoulder, and with ears outspread, ten feet one inch from tip to tip. We started a man for camp at once for an axe to cut out the ivory and porters to carry it in. Then we sat down, made a cup of tea and gazed at the elephant.

The native shambas with their little grass huts, looking like haystacks set in green fields of maize, broke the monotony of the trip down the river.

Dugouts, guided by natives, carried loads upstream.

Three hours later the axe arrived. It is said to be bad luck to carry one with you when hunting. With the porters, came a swarm of natives for the meat. We cut off the forefeet, a piece of hide four by six feet, an ear, the tail and started chopping out the tusks. This was a three-hour job so that it was after 4 p.m. when we started for camp five miles away. By the time we arrived, the excitement had passed and we were just tired out.

The hunt was over and we had only to return to our base at Saga for the run across the desert. We broke camp early the next day and loaded our duffle into catamarans, which we made by lashing two dugouts together.

Our drift downriver twenty miles promised to be a lovely rest as the river was beautiful - green banks with overhanging trees. The native shambas with their little grass huts, looking like hay stacks set in green fields of maize, broke the monotony. The inhabitants came out and shouted greetings to our men and an animated conversation of grunts and yells was continued as long as we were in sight. Monkeys swished in the trees where the forest had not been cut back for maize fields and flocks of goats, white sheep with black heads, and camels were constantly appearing at the water's edge.

It had all the elements of a lovely picture and so it was until ten hours of it had passed and we were thoroughly broiled sitting in the blazing sun. We reached camp at 6 p.m. and I never saw a place more welcome.

On the run across the desert for the first sixty miles we made good time (averaging thirteen miles per hour). Then we saw a motor car in the road ahead and, as we drew alongside, it proved to be Aloo and our six-wheel truck. We had told this fool Kavirondo to wait for us at Garba Tulla but he decided to push on and had broken down miles from any place. He had been there two days and had just finished drinking the last of the water in the radiator when we arrived. We were so mad we could hardly see but we took him in tow and traveled on another fifty-six miles (total 116) to the first water. Here we camped.

The next day we pushed on thirty-three miles to the Kina River (elevation 2,550 feet), where we left the men to make camp while we strolled up a hill not far from camp that rose three or four hundred feet above the plain. From the top we looked over a lot of country and within a radius of three miles spotted eight rhino. That was good enough and we decided to give this part of the country a day's hunt and look over these fellows at closer range. We were away the next day as soon as it

Overhanging trees and monkeys swishing in the branches added to the atmosphere of the place as Prent and Percival drifted downriver.

was light enough to shoot. I had been told that it was not safe in rhino country to wander about in the bush while it was still dark. Africa is full of "don'ts."

We climbed the same hill and began seeing rhino in all directions. We counted nine and laid out a march that would let us inspect most of them at close range. Just as we were about to descend, a cow and calf rhino came over the top of the hill and gave us quite a fright as we did not see them till they were within thirty yards. Then we slipped in behind some rocks and got a hundred feet of movies of them before they moved off. As we came down the hill, we put up a bunch of six lions but there was not a "wooly" one with them and we let them go.

Approaching our first rhino nearly made a nervous wreck of me as we walked up to within forty yards. The rhino had a poor head and we passed on. We looked over twelve in this way, sometimes single ones, sometimes two together, once three under the shade of the same tree. Always we approached within fifty yards and only one caught our wind and made off. Most of them had poor heads until we came to two sleeping under a thorn tree. One of these had the best horn we had seen although it was nothing to write home about. After much discussion, we decided to kill it and end the rhino business.

The approach was out in the open with no cover and at sixty yards the tick birds flew off the rhino's back and it was on its feet like a shot. I had to fire hurriedly but the bullet took it square in the shoulder and by all rules it was a dead rhino. However, the rhino whirled and started off. The second barrel broke its pelvis as it ran straight away from us and the rhino was anchored. Nevertheless, it took six more .465 shells all in the chest cavity before it was down. The second rhino was not at all inclined to leave and we thought we had a party on our hands as the rhino kept dashing about with its tail in the air. However, finally the rhino left and we went in to find our horn measured only sixteen and a half inches. We took the scalp and the forefeet and told the men they could have the hide, which pleased them more than five shillings apiece.

We decided to devote a day with the cameras trying for rhino pictures, and a short distance from camp we found an old fellow that gave us a certain amount of film before it caught our wind and fled. We worked on and came on a cow and calf but they persisted in standing in fairly high grass and finally lay down to sleep.

Then a solitary bull came, causing a great snorting on the part of all three until they looked each other over carefully and laid down for a nap. This did us no good

A giraffe peers above the brush.

photographically, so we sent a boy upwind to stir them up. They caught his scent while the boy was still 200 yards away and were on their feet in an instant. The next moment they were trotting off rapidly.

We had now only one more animal we particularly wanted to get - a Cape buffalo - and so moved camp a few miles. An early start seems to be a requisite in buffalo hunting so we tramped off through the long grass just at dawn. For six long hours we plowed through rank buffalo grass five or six feet tall in which we could not see more than a few feet ahead. I was scared to death and nearly gibbering. A rhino snorted at us not far off and we gave his apparent position a wide berth, although we never saw him. We did, however, see three other rhino in time to avoid them and five elephants. Finally, two bull Cape buffalo burst out of the grass and tore away. I had a running shot at about 150 yards as they topped a little rise but missed.

When we made camp at noon we decided we had had enough of this and would move into some place that had been burned off. We moved camp thirty miles toward Meru to a place called Ayres Corner.

We were camped at an elevation of more than 5,000 feet and for the first time in two weeks slept under blankets. The country was gorgeous. We were up in the foothills of Mount Kenya and the flat desert appearance of the country had disappeared. Numerous small streams ran down to the plain and their banks were lined by tall mimosa trees.

To cap it all, we had a view of the mountain itself. Not a very clear view but for a time in the early morning we could see the two peaks and for even that we were thankful as seldom is it clear of clouds.

We hunted hard from daylight till noon and saw nothing except one rhino and some eland. Our way led through swamps where the reeds were over our heads and I did not care for it at all. One could not see two feet in any direction.

We were out again at four and scoured the country without seeing a Cape buffalo. As we came back toward camp we saw a very good rhino; much better, in fact, than anything we had seen and, after a council of war, it was decided to take the rhino on my second license. I fired twice at sixty yards and it wheeled and gaily galloped into the reeds. I had another glimpse at something over 100 yards and hit again, but as it did not come out on the far bank we concluded the rhino was down and we would have to go into the tall grass for it.

Posing with Prent's rhinoceros is Philip Percival and native guides. They had counted nine animals but this male had the largest horn.

It was no place at all for Mrs. Gray's eldest male child, as the reeds were tall and thick as mush. However, after an hour's search, Percival found the rhino dead as mutton and we were tremendously relieved. The rhino's horn measured nineteen inches in length and 21-1/4 inches around the base.

We went out the next morning without a great deal of hope, but rather than lose a day entirely we thought to make a short hunt while the boys were breaking camp and to return about 10 a.m. and move to Embu where Cape buffalo were reported to be numerous.

About 7 a.m. we spied a Cape buffalo a long way off and our stalk was so successful we came out within fifty yards. It was a cow and a small one at that. The Cape buffalo cow fled into a swampy patch of reed about ten acres in extent.

We could not figure out what a cow was doing there all alone so decided to burn the reeds and see what appeared. We sat up on a side hill and sent the boys downwind to start the fires. It made slow headway but suddenly we saw the reeds sway, some tick birds flew up and slowly three cows and two calves made their way to the edge of the swamp. We could not see the animals, only the swaying reeds, until they emerged. Our hearts fell as we had been following their progress full of hope. A half-hour passed and then two old cows burst out. We had not even seen them move in the swamp. We waited and prayed for a bull.

Finally, we gave it up as the fire seemed to have about cleaned up all the grass. We started for camp but in one corner of the swamp across which we were headed I caught just an impression of some animal in a little clump of reeds. The others said I was seeing things but we called to the boys to fire this little patch. Before they could light a match, the bull caught their wind and came crashing out in our direction. I had to wait precious seconds until Percival was sure it was a bull and then I emptied my Springfield into the bull at about fifty yards as it tore along through the tall grass. The bull kept going and I ran after it reloading as I went. As the bull came out into an opening I fired three more shots to see it go down.

Now we had a new trouble. The Cape buffalo lay right in the path of the fire. We put one more shot into the bull to be sure it would stay down, and started a back fire around its body. We thus saved the slightly singed skin. Four of the shots were just where they should have been in the shoulder and one was in its neck. The last was too far back in its side to do much immediate harm. The bull was a splendid specimen, 42-1/2 inches across, with an enormous boss measuring thirteen

The Meru buffalo guide in a resting attitude,
forty miles south of Meru, Kenya.

Waterbuck take a drink.

inches wide.

I thanked the Lord this was over for, frankly, I had been scared to death by these Cape buffalo. As I stood looking down on its enormous bulk I believe I had reason to be scared. They are crafty, fast and terrifically powerful, besides weighing over 2,000 pounds and living in the most difficult country to hunt - long grass.

On our way back to camp we saw sixteen elephants feeding quite a way off but they held no interest, for my hunting in Kenya was over. I was tremendously proud of the way my leg had behaved. It was troublesome at night after a long day but it carried me through till the Cape buffalo was down.

We returned to camp to make the men unpack, sent four porters to carry in the Cape buffalo head and sat back to perfect comfort and rest. I felt a sort of distinction in not having been charged by a single animal, not even a dik-dik. Few American hunters admit this.

We drove the twenty-three miles to Meru quite early, passing a herd of twenty elephants feeding in the open but not far from the forest. We put in a couple of hours photographing the natives about the market place, which filled in the time till it was proper for us to arrive at Pat Ayre's house for lunch. Here we picked up Bowen, who had collected a lot of excellent forest birds.

The bird life of the forest of Mount Kenya was unlike any previously encountered, and hence of great interest. By far the most plentiful were the several species of forest bulbuls. These were all dull colored and inconspicuous, except insofar as their numbers were concerned. Yellow and black orioles were abundant and conspicuous. The noisy, but beautiful Hartlaub's turaco, with deep green body and blue crest, crept about amidst the thick foliage, inconspicuous until it flew, when the bright red wings flashed out. Their noisy calls were heard at all times. A dull-colored spur-fowl ran about in the undergrowth, and the beautiful blue-spotted crested guinea fowl was heard more often than seen. Two species of hornbills occurred; one, a large bird, was nearly three feet in length with an enormous yellowish casque covering almost the whole length of the bill. Its loud honking call resounded through the forest.

By far the most beautiful bird of the forest was the narina trogon with crimson breast and emerald green back. This and its cousin, the bar-tailed trogon, were seen several times sitting motionless on some conspicuous branch. Large forked-tailed drongoes darted down upon unsuspecting insects and returned to devour their prey

Percival rests beside the Cape buffalo that measured 42-1/2 inches across with an enormous boss measuring 13 inches wide.

upon some conspicuous perch. Beautiful yellow-throated, green bee-eaters, long-tailed red-backed paradise flycatchers and other and less conspicuous flycatchers were to be seen on all sides capturing insects upon the wing.

A black and white barbet with a large powerful bill was common and its call, which sounded like, "Ho, ho, ho," was always answered (probably by the female) with a single, "Ha," in a higher pitch. Doves of several species were common.

In the evening when the safari ants become active, certain species of birds came down in numbers to feed upon them. Amongst these was the beautiful little white-starred bush-robin, the male of which is bright yellow below, olive green above with a slaty grey head. On either side of the forehead and upon the throat are spots of pearly white, looking like jewels.

In the open country below the forest, chats and babblers were common. Sunbirds frequented the flowering shrubs and the beautiful amethyst starling abounded. Two species of okpeckers perched upon the backs of game and native cattle alike, searching for ticks. Bowen found three new subspecies here, a kingfisher that he named *Halcyon albiventris prentissgrayi,* and a starling named *Cinnyricinclus leucogaster lauragrayae,* and a barbet named *Smilorhis leucotis kenyae.*

This same afternoon we pulled on fifty-seven miles to Nanyuki, which sits astride the equator. Despite this we and all the men were nearly frozen before we arrived there at 8 p.m.

The next day's drive of 102 miles lay through a beautiful country after we passed Nyeri. We did not want to arrive in Nairobi at night so pulled up at the Blue Post Hotel at Thika, thirty-two miles from Nairobi.

We had a week to wait for our steamer to Dar es Salaam so we decided to photograph in the southern game reserve. It always seemed an endless struggle to get out of Nairobi. We had to put off our departure for three days because the men were missing. Finally, we moved out to Percival's farm at Machakos where we met Blayney Percival and negotiated the purchase of his bird collection for the Philadelphia Academy of Natural Sciences. Then we drove on to a railroad station at Kui where we spent the night in the station house.

We turned in early but some Kikuyu natives working on the railroad decided to have a dance. After fighting against the unearthly monotonous noise of the drums for an hour we went out to watch this weird sight of black naked bodies writhing before the fire in time to their chant.

Meru girls

We drove on into the Masai Game Reserve and soon began to see herds of cattle and an occasional manyata or native village. After fifteen miles we came to a dry riverbed at a place called Mashuru, where the cattle were watered at holes dug in the sand. From these holes water is dipped and poured into clay troughs from which the cattle drink. Most of the day this goes on till the cattle are driven to the manyatas for the night. Then the game gets a chance at the water.

We dug a hole about eight feet square in the sandy first bench of the river and stretched a piece of canvas in front of it. We pushed the lenses of our cameras through holes in the canvas and, crawling down into the hole, prepared to await the game.

It was a hot business as the sun poured down on us mercilessly and what direct rays missed us were reflected back by the white sand. Flies swarmed about us and it was hard not to wave our arms to drive them away. Motion was the one thing we had to avoid for the game approached the drinking place on the high bank above us and the slightest movement would send them hurrying away.

Almost on the tick of 4 p.m. we saw the first game - a herd of zebra on the bank behind us about 200 yards away. They looked the water hole over carefully for so long I thought they must suspect our presence. They were ill-natured brutes for we could see them fighting continually among themselves, kicking and biting; a succession of squeals reached our ears.

Finally, they decided to drink and in single file came down the bank and straight up the sandy riverbed. They ignored the water hole in front of our blind and passed us forty yards away for other holes just upstream but which were hardly within camera range. We took a few pictures, however, and then turned our attention to the sand grouse that were coming in considerable numbers for their evening drink. They were restless birds that insisted on flitting from one water hole to another, never taking but a sip at any one place.

We had not long to wait before a herd of impala appeared but they watered 200 yards downstream from us and only one doe came to our water hole. When they left it was after sunset and, dismounting the camera, we made our way back to camp.

We loafed the next morning away except to take some pictures of the Masai watering their cattle and the women dipping the water from holes dug in the sandy riverbed and pouring it into troughs of clay.

Zebra graze at a water hole.

After a sumptuous lunch (These were our last days in camp and many odds and ends like canned asparagus had to be eaten.), we drove to an Indian trading post five miles away to photograph some of the Masai we figured would be there. We had no success until we bought a dozen strings of beads, then all the native belles wanted their picture taken. One 25 cent (Kenya cents) string of beads for as many pictures as we wished of the subject was the price and we wasted a lot of film.

At 4 p.m. Percival and I crawled into the blind and we hardly settled down before some zebra appeared. They posed for us nicely at sixty yards and to our great delight brought three wildebeest along with them.

After we had all we wished of this, two wart hogs came down to rout out a hole in the sand with their snouts and quench their thirst. Their heads, for most part, were below the level of the sand so they did not make good pictures until they trotted off with their funny tails straight up in the air.

On the way back to Percival's ranch, we photographed a Masai manyata. I have never seen so many flies in my life. The faces of the natives crawled with them and while I had a boy swishing them off my face while I worked the camera, I nearly went crazy with them. It took us ten miles to get them out of the car after we left.

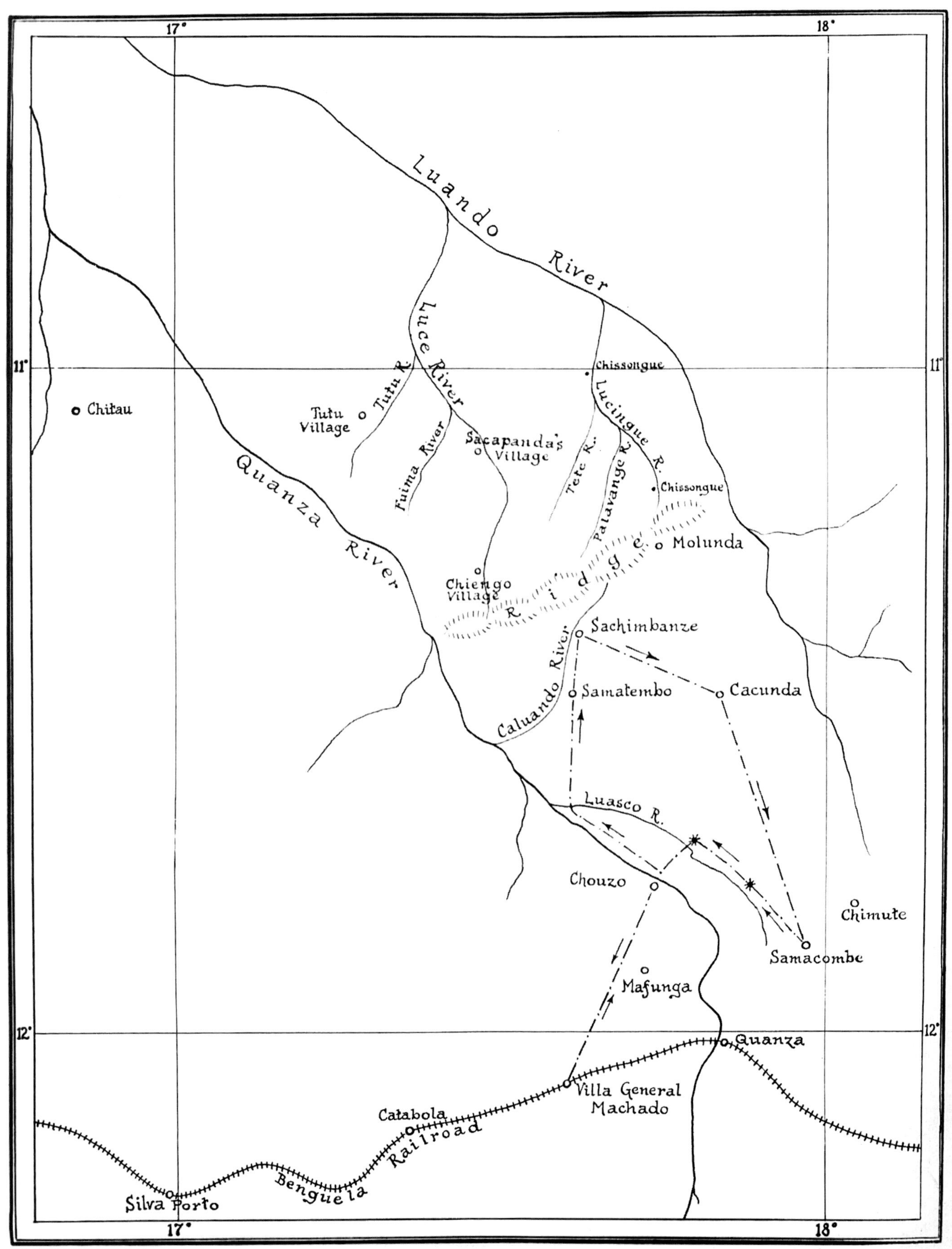

A map drawn by Prentiss N. Gray shows the territory covered along and between the Luando and Quanza rivers. Stars drawn on the map show specimen collection points.

ANGOLA

PART FOUR

ALONG THE LIVINGSTONE TRAIL

ON August 19th we said our last farewells to our kind friends in Kenya, especially the Percivals, and two days later sailed out of Mombasa Harbor on the "S.S. Aviateur Roland Garros," a frightful old tub. However bad the boat, it could neither spoil the wonderful moonlight or later, the view of Zanzibar as we steamed by close in shore. The next morning we were off Dar es Salaam and, picking up the pilot, went in through the narrow entrance. On the southern point was a floating dry dock that during the war the Germans sank across the entrance, effectually keeping the British fleet out.

Dar es Salaam is a lovely spot - good substantial buildings, a beautiful harbor, clean streets and a distinct air of prosperity. Its officials, however, were as slow and tiresome as in most places. People are always slow and tiresome when you are in a hurry.

I decided as soon as I got ashore to take a goods train up to Dodoma and have one day's hunt for greater kudu. The train left at 11 a.m., one hour after we reached the shore. It was a mad race between the police office and the customs house to clear the guns and get permission to ride on the goods train.

Finally, with very little baggage and no food, I landed in a third-class carriage with a lot of natives and Indians and we started. I had my bed roll and appropriated one end of the carriage, putting up my ground cloth as a screen. I sat down on the hard board seat for the twenty-five hour journey and, incidentally, to starve.

Morning without a wash and no breakfast was not very cheerful but we arrived at Dodoma at noon and I splashed and ate to make up for it.

Kudu fawn

Kudu

Dodoma is situated on the divide between the Indian Ocean and the East African Rift Valley, a great trough that cuts the granite plateau from 6 degrees south latitude northward through the Red Sea into the Valley of the Dead Sea and the Jordan to the foot of Lebanon.

The town is 254 miles from the coast and stands at an elevation of 3,670 feet above the sea. The country about looks pretty thoroughly dried out and barren but it is inhabited by a pastoral tribe of natives called Wagogo, who resemble the Masai in their general appearance and habits of life except they build flat-roofed rectangular houses wherein numerous families and all the goats and cattle live together. We were particularly struck by the number of melons laid out on the flat roofs to boil in the sun until they are rotten and then eaten with great gusto.

About 3 p.m. I hired a motor truck to drive me fifteen miles out of town to some brushy hills. At a native village I persuaded a couple of savages to show me where to find kudu. They started me off at a run, which they kept up until 6 p.m. Arriving back at the truck I was completely tired out while they were as fresh as daisies. We never saw a sign of kudu.

The driver of the motor truck called me at 4 a.m. the next day and we started forth. There was a distinct chill in the air but, as we thought of the sweltering heat of this sandy plain at noon, was welcome. All the country around Dodoma was dry as a bone and although the natives raised cattle and goats, it was hard to see what they lived on in this sandy, rocky waste.

We found two native boys who knew just where kudu were to be found in great numbers and I will say for them that my ankle injury had some slight effect on their speed and as a result we came within good range of three kudu cows. I nearly put my eyes out trying to make horns grow on one. When I let all three go, the boys fairly wept.

I remembered the advice of Blayney Percival[1] when he said, "I have hunted kudu thirty years and have only learned to go half slow enough."

However, you can't slow down a native and my efforts only persuaded them that I tired easily. After each stop to look over the country, they would tear on till I insisted on stopping again.

[1] Blayney Percival served as a game warden in Kenya for twenty-two years and authored a book about wildlife of Africa titled, *A Game Ranger on Safari*, published in 1928.

Wagogo natives

We drove back to Dodoma for lunch and made a fresh start at 3 p.m. I previously had been hunting the hills to the west of the Iringa Road and for the last hunt I decided to try the eastern side. I had the same nine-year-old native boy for a guide and he had brought along two other little fellows even smaller than himself.

We had been out about an hour when I heard a crash in the bush above me and ran ahead to a little open space from which I could see up onto a rocky hillside. I caught a glimpse of several animals moving through the thick bush and as one passed a small opening I saw it was a bull kudu. I fired offhand and the dispatch with which it appeared from behind the bush told me I had hit. The bull kept on, however, and I caught only occasional glimpses of the kudu through the thorn trees and among the big rocks with which the steep hillside was strewn. Three other bulls, which had broken cover at the same time, complicated the situation as I could not be sure which was the one I had already wounded and I did not want to kill two.

Finally, I caught a glimpse of one with a patch of blood on its shoulder and I fired to see the bull come down with a crash. It was a tremendous relief because I was really trying to do something in one day that everybody told me would take at least two weeks.

I was very much surprised at the size of the greater kudu when I got up to this fellow. The greater kudu was considerably larger than a wildebeest and I should estimate it weighed close to 600 pounds. This particular animal did not have a big head as far as the records go, measuring forty-five inches, but it seemed to me a magnificent trophy and the mealless, waterless ride up from Dar es Salaam (even the frightful meals at the Greek Dodoma Hotel) were more than balanced off as I saw it lying before me.

I had a hard job getting the kudu's head off as I could not turn it over alone, but finally I succeeded and carried it down the hill a couple of miles to the road.

I spent most of the night skinning out the head and often I longed for Hamesi of our northern safari days who seemed to pull off head skins as if it was no work at all.

From Dodoma the railroad followed quite closely the old Arab trade route along which so much white and black ivory was brought to the coast during the last century. Most of the main towns such as Kilosa and Tabora were old Arab strongholds, built to secure their line of communication between the coast and the great

Luimbi medicine men were asked to cast a spell over sable antelope so Prentiss would have good luck during the hunt.

lakes of Central Africa.

The route had other memories. Just out of Tabora at Kwihara, Stanley and Livingstone lived together in 1872 and not far off was the pass between two hills where they parted. At the end of our rail journey at Ujiji, on the lake stood the old mango tree under which they met in 1871. It was the romance of this old trail that led me to cross Africa from east to west before the tourists spoiled it, rather than the Cape to Cairo route on which Thos. Cook & Sons now runs tours.

A day later we arrived at Kigoma on Lake Tanganyika and started the tedious business of clearing the Tanganyika customs outgoing and entering the Belgian Congo. On the eastern side of the lake the Belgians, under the Treaty of Versailles, have a free port and for the convenience of passengers customs formalities can be complied with here.

It was bad enough getting out of Tanganyika and getting back our gun deposit through the usual stupid Indian clerk. We anticipated untold difficulties with the Belgians. However, a letter from Ex-Governor General Lippens, which Millard Shaler[2] obtained for me, smoothed the way and our thirty-three pieces of baggage expeditiously moved onto the "S.S. Liemba."

The "S.S. Liemba" was a trim little ship built by the Germans just before the war and sunk in the lake at the end of hostilities. The British raised her and refitted her very well. We made the run of eighty miles across the lake during the night and at daylight were anchored off Albertville.

Greatly to our surprise, District Commissioner Raffaele Caroli was at the dock to meet us and had a gang of convicts, chained together by the neck, carry our baggage to the hotel. We spent all day, however, telling our life history to the immigration authorities and obtaining a permit to carry arms. I was heartbroken when they insisted on stamping their registration numbers into the stock of every gun and then having the nerve to charge us fifty francs each for so defacing them. However, it was finally over and the district commissioner took us off to his home for a sundowner and a gorgeous dinner.

We left on the train for Kabalo the next morning and the district commissioner

[2] In 1917, during World War I, Millard Shaler worked closely with Prentiss Gray in Herbert Hoover's Commission for Relief of Belgium. Shaler married a Belgian woman and remained in Brussels in business during the 1920s. Thus, he knew many Belgian government officials who could assist Prentiss Gray.

Prentiss had many opportunities to photograph Luimbi natives. The men served as porters and some showed abilities as trackers.

was at the station to see us off. We had a lot to thank Shaler for in arranging all this courtesy from officials.

The country on the western side of the lake was much more attractive than Tanganyika. There was not the dried-up desert appearance and in places it was covered with good trees clear of underbrush. Completing a run of 190 miles, we rolled into Kabalo, after following the valley of the Lukuga River through which Lake Tanganyika empties itself periodically. Kabalo was not much to look at, consisting of a brick railway station, two tin-roofed stores, two whitewashed residences apparently of the white railroad officials and a small native village. Apparently there was a jail some place, for the usual prisoners - chained together by the neck - were on hand to unload the mail. We had a very good dinner in the station and about 8 p.m. the "S.S. Louis Cousin" hove in sight coming up the Lualaba River. It took some time to offload the part of her cargo destined for Dar es Salaam and I counted forty elephant tusks came ashore. All, however, were very small and the heaviest could not have exceeded twenty-five pounds.

It was after 10 p.m. before we were settled aboard and as we were pretty tired we were soon inside our mosquito nets and asleep. Sometime before it was light the ship started and when we awoke we were steaming up the Lualaba, which is really the Upper Congo. It was here a stream about 200 yards wide and eight to ten feet deep. At this time of year the water was very low and everyone anticipated we would spend a certain length of time sitting on sandbars before we reached Bukama, 400 miles away.

From the upper deck, even at this low stage of water, we could see out onto the flats beyond. A fringe of palms and green trees, of course, lined the banks but beyond these were a greater number of green trees than I had seen anywhere in East Africa except on the slopes of Mount Kenya. The natives were dressed in European clothes and Kabalo reminded me more of a Louisiana levee than the heart of the Congo. This, to my mind, is one of the crimes of the missionaries, for they have foolishly taught the native he must wear clothes but cannot put European standards of modesty into his mind to go with them.

I had been struck by the tremendous brick buildings called missions all along the line since we left Albertville. Never again will I waste sympathy on the poor missionary in darkest Africa. Most of the churches in small native villages would grace a city of ten thousand people at home.

All afternoon we steamed through rather uninteresting country. As evening came, the game began to appear and the captain stopped the ship to fire ten shots at a bunch of antelope. He hit one but as it appeared to be traveling strong the captain did not go after it. A mile farther the captain stopped again and after firing seventeen shots, crippled five and following them, killed two small females. Soon we stopped again and a fusilade of shots, which I lost count of after twelve, produced at least one cripple that the boys drove out of the reeds to the captain on shore. He killed it in three more shots at twenty yards. This was another female. The whole business was nauseating. If this shooting from steamers, even on the excuse that it provides meat for passengers, is continued there will not be a head of game left in the country. The miserable shooting and the failure to follow-up cripples but to shoot another animal is criminal.

At 9 p.m. we stopped at Muyumba, which is the shipping port for the tin mines of Manono. Some few whites and the usual horde of natives appeared to welcome the steamer. The slope down to the river was very steep but it was surprising to note the difficulty the natives had in getting up and down the bank. Even a white woman with high-heeled shoes handled the steep slope better than the natives, who all agreed have a fear of high or steep places.

The ship ran all through the night although I confess I could not understand how the officer on the bridge could see the banks.

The captain gave us another exhibition of shooting early the next morning but this time, out of the herd at less than a hundred yards, a buck dropped. The skipper

"S.S. Louis Cousin" took them down the Lualaba River. Prent counted a total of 40 elephant tusks being unloaded at Kabalo where he boarded.

was as surprised as any of us as he had only fired four shots.

All day long we traveled through a low-lying country, which offered nothing of special interest, but it was better than the day following when for all the daylight hours we plowed through a huge papyrus swamp. As far as we could see were nothing but the huge feathery tops of the reeds, the river cutting a narrow channel through the sea of green. Crocodiles became a common sight and the bird life was astounding. Many small birds were seen, such as little bee-eaters, swallows, wagtails and small sandpipers, but the outstanding feature of the bird life seen during this trip was the immense numbers of large water birds. Goliath herons, large as their name implies, stood solitarily fishing in the shallow water; several other herons and egrets were common too. Snake-birds, so called on account of their long snake-like head and neck, abounded everywhere, and long-tailed cormorants were nearly as numerous.

By far the most numerous bird was the open-billed stork, a large blackish bird with peculiar bill that leaves a gap between the mandibles in the middle part. These abounded everywhere, crowding trees along the banks, until there was room for not a single other bird. Sandbanks along the way were literally black with the species, and the sky was full of them circling overhead.

Upon other sandbanks rested numerous spur-winged and Egyptian geese and several species of plover. The African skimmer (rather like the American species) was common, too, and was thought to be breeding.

River eagles, with black bodies and white heads, looking remarkably like the American eagle, were common everywhere, as were also crested eagles and vulturine fish eagles.

The vegetation along the banks teemed with small land birds, but identification of these from the decks of the steamer was often impossible.

The river became very tortuous and for hours there was not a straight stretch a hundred yards long. A few native villages occurred on the banks and it was evident from the smell their inhabitants were engaged in fishing.

After dark we pulled up at a small village called Kiabo where, we were told, we must change to a smaller steamer as the water in the river was too low for our vessel to continue. The next day a small paddle wheel boat came alongside and we were hustled aboard, bag and baggage. There was no place to sit out of the sun except the bridge and too many of us to all squeeze in there. Bowen and I, therefore,

The Lualaba River

Young boys greeted the steamer along the river banks at Muyumba.
Muyumba was the shipping port for the tin mines of Manono.

climbed to the top of the pilot house where we set up the Akeley camera and hoped, in spite of the vibration, to get some bird pictures as we traveled along.

It was a long, hot, monotonous day and the sun had baked us through and through before we arrived. Our only diversion besides the camera was shooting crocodiles, which were fairly numerous, and giving advice how to get off sandbars on which we were constantly sticking.

At last, just after sunset, we arrived at Bukama, which was a terrible place to reach at any time of day and when you have had no lunch and hope for a good dinner, it is a hopeless outlook. The administrator of the place met us on instructions from the governor general but he was thoroughly drunk and had no idea where we were to sleep. The hotel consisted of four rooms and a bar and there were twenty passengers. Finally, the Greek who ran the hotel produced a really good dinner and that cheered our souls.

We were due to leave by train for Elizabethville at midday but the train was very late and it was not until 5:30 p.m. that we departed. The administrator came down to see us off at noon and stayed on, getting drunk, until by train time he could hardly walk. He did, however, have some prisoners carry our baggage to the station.

Bowen preferred to stay at Bukama while I traveled to Elizabethville to arrange the Angola trip. The region looked good from a bird's point of view and I planned to meet him in Tshilongo in a week.

On arrival at Elizabethville I found, however, that the Benguella Railroad only ran a train every ten days to the border and that to catch it I could only tarry two days. I, therefore, had but little time to see the district as I wanted but did look over one mine and enjoyed the modern comforts of Elizabethville after several weeks of travel. It was the most modern town I had seen in Africa. Well-paved streets, large stone buildings, spacious parks and attractive houses all surprised me and made me want to stay longer with delightful friends to get the real atmosphere of the place.

I had engaged a motor to take us via Tshilongo to Dilolo Gare on the Angola frontier. It was to leave the hotel at 6 a.m. and at that hour I was seated on top of my luggage in front of the hotel. No car arrived and at 8 a.m. I went off to see why. I was met with a lot of conversation about breakdowns but surely it would be ready at 10 a.m. At 11 a.m. it would be ready at noon and at 1 p.m. it would be all in order to start at 4 p.m.

About noon I called on the director of the railroad, M. Gilet, and told him my

The river cut a narrow channel through a sea of green.

troubles. He most kindly offered to get me a motor at Tshilongo and to take me there (a ten-hour run) in his private car on the railroad. I accepted eagerly and so at 5:30 p.m. when the local garage representative arrived to tell me he was finally ready, I had a joyful moment telling him to go to hell.

At 9 p.m. we left Elizabethville in the director's private car, which had been built for the King and Queen of Belgium when they came out in 1928 to open the new railway line from Port Francqui to Bukama. A large gilt plaque attested to the fact I was drinking my whiskey and soda seated on the Queen's couch and when I crawled into bed I was informed this was the same bed the Queen had slept in. It was a cinch it was not the one Albert had used - not by at least a foot - and if to posterity they tell the tale that P. Gray slept therein they will be plain liars because I never slept a wink. It was too short to stretch out in and too narrow to double up. I was most uncomfortable.

However, a good breakfast evened it up and at 9:30 a.m. we arrived at Tshilongo. Bowen, perched on all the luggage, was there looking thoroughly disconsolate as he had been put off the train at midnight in this little town that had no hotel. He had slept by the railroad track and gone without breakfast. When I rolled up in a private car and told him of luscious paw-paws and scrambled eggs for breakfast, it did not help any. Our motorcar was nearly ready and with only three hours more delay we were off. We had a belated lunch at Musonoi, which is now only a little village of one store and a few native huts but is destined soon to be the center of a large group of mines. The Union Miniere have started to open up twenty-two mines in this vicinity and the smelter and main works will be at Musonoi. We stopped for the night at the rest house erected by Robert Williams Co. at Mulomba - 162 kilometers, or 100 miles from Tshilongo. The road had been fair most of the way but the country was uninteresting. A high plateau (1,300 meters) was covered with scrubby timber that shuts off all the view. Game was a thing of the past. In all this distance I saw only one antelope.

We put in another long day covering 130 miles. It would not be long on American roads but it took us from 7:30 a.m. to 5 p.m. steady going. We saw not a single head of game in a country that we were told once fairly crawled with it till the Belgians shot it all.

As we traveled farther away from the railroad and farther from the missions, the natives appeared more nearly in their native state. Since we entered the Congo, all

A basket is created.

we have seen have been natives more thoroughly dressed in European clothes than the Negroes of the cotton fields of our South. Here we saw a few still without shirts or shorts.

We pulled into Luashi to spend the night at another rest house and they did us very well. Several times during the day we had been ferried across rivers on a float resting on four or five dugout canoes. They looked too flimsy to take the motor car, as they were simply a floor of poles tied to the canoes with strips of bark. The ferry men are the disseminators of news and gossip for the countryside, and accidents of embarkation are the highlights of their lives, throwing them into a positive frenzy of jubilation. We crossed one bridge forty meters long that did not have a nail in it. At the high point it was fifty feet above the riverbed and as the bark ties that fastened it together had loosened in the dry weather, the bridge swayed with the weight of the car. I thought surely it was going to fall apart but we reached the other side safely.

It looked for a time the next morning as if our transport man had left us in the middle of Africa. He did not put in an appearance and as he had collected 7,800 francs from us the night before, we feared he had deserted us. However, it was only the Belgian idea of being on time (three hours late) and I found him two miles down the road fixing another motorcar.

We covered the remaining 110 miles to Dilolo Gare before 4 p.m. We found a busy new town. Buildings of brick, even though thatch-roofed, were going up all over the place. It had all the air of a boom town of our West except the streets were well laid out and the buildings of a more permanent character. We were put up at the railroad rest house and very comfortably taken care of.

We had a busy morning getting our guns out of the Belgian customs and searching for the permit to shoot giant sable, which was supposed to be waiting for us. It was no place to be found so we crossed the Luano River into Portuguese Angola and drove eight miles to the town of Vila Teixeira de Sousa in search of Major Torre de Valle, who was reported to have it

He was easily found but had never heard of us or the permit. However, he took us to the customs and started the elaborate procedure of entering our guns into Angola. As this is a penal colony it is a most difficult matter and we had heard discouraging tales of months spent in vain effort to get the guns back after the Portuguese once had their hands on them. Nine months wait was the least we had

Natives appeared more nearly in their native state.

been told about. We had, therefore, left our guns in Belgian territory and gone over to discuss the matter first.

We had just made a good start in the conversation when the customs officer seemed to remember a telegram with my name in it and a diligent search produced a message dated early in June from the governor general telling the border officials to give us every facility and allow us free entry. This was a tremendous relief and soon all the papers were in order. Bowen drove back to Dilolo but I waited, as I had heard the governor of the province was on the incoming train and I hoped he might know where our shooting permit was.

The train, which leaves Lobito every two weeks, arrived about 5 p.m. and after a very formal presentation to the governor of the district I broached the subject of our permit. Yes, he had been advised of our coming and he knew there was such a permit but just where it was he could not remember.

I was disconsolate because, in addition, there was no word from Evans[3] as to where we were to leave the train or whether he had arranged our safari.

However, I was determined to go on and fight it out. So I took the train back to Dilolo Gare and arrived there to find Bowen in a panic because he could not buy an angolar (the monetary unit of Angola) and the station agent would not sell us a ticket with anything but angolars. We went to bed far from happy.

We were up with the dawn to hunt angolars and by train time I had, with difficulty, located some and had purchased enough to take us on our journey. Porters moved our baggage across the river to the Portuguese side, as the train does not run across the river. The Belgians and the Portuguese cannot agree on which side the customs house is to be located. This will probably take several years to resolve.

However, at the terminus we found Major Torre de Valle and he told us our permit had arrived in the mail. He had left his office in such a hurry to catch the train that he had forgotten it. Possibly if we talked nicely to the conductor he would hold the train at Teixeira de Sousa long enough for him to send to his office for it. Much pleasant talk and some bribery had the desired effect and just as the conductor was getting impatient the long-hunted papers arrived.

Imagine our chagrin when we opened the precious document to find it allowed

[3] Sherman Gray said that in a later writing of his father, Prentiss explained that J.R. Evans was an American living in Angola who had received cables from Prentiss over a six month period. "Later we learned he had received all our cables but his replies had never reached us," Prentiss wrote.

The barber shop

us to shoot only two giant sable. It was impossible to make a group of two and we were mad clear through after our long trip across Africa. There was no letter from Evans but Torre de Valle advised us to leave the train at a station called General Machado (Camacupa) where we were due the following morning.

His Excellency, the Governor of the District of Moxico, Vasco Lopes Alves, boarded the train and over a glass of beer proved a very sympathetic listener to our lament. He was returning to the capital at Vila Sousa and might be useful in keeping us out of jail.

We arrived at General Machado (Camacupa) at 9:40 a.m. and our hearts sank as we saw no Evans waiting for us on the platform. We did see a sign, "Hotel," and there we landed our baggage after a verbal struggle with the proprietor who spoke nothing but Portuguese. Finally, he led us to the store of Santos Cunha & Co. where a clerk knew a smattering of French. By writing out what we wanted in French we got our thoughts over to him - even if laboriously - and he trotted us around to the Chef de Posto, who fortunately had a letter from the governor about us and nearly broke his neck to render assistance. We sent off telegrams to every place that Evans could possibly be and finally received word that he would arrive late that night by motor.

After lunch, Machado, the Chef de Posto, drove us twenty-one miles, to the Quanza River, where we had our first view of the promised land where we hoped to find the giant sable. We stood on the high river bank at the native village of Chouzo and looked out across the river flats to a low range of hills covered with brush, which was the only place in the world where this rare antelope is found.

The natives here are Luimbi, a tribe never famous for industry or agricultural proficiency. We also concluded that the women would win no blue ribbons in a beauty contest but the men served us well as porters and some of them showed ability as trackers. Chouzo was one of their largest villages and, located on the high bank of the river, commanded a splendid view across the marshes to the height of land between the Quanza and the Loando rivers. Like all the old native villages in Angola, the houses were built in a grove of mulemba trees, which towered far above the surrounding scrub. The houses of the chief and his immediate family of three wives occupied the center of the village. Their huts were surrounded by a stockade of heavy twelve-foot posts with but a single doorway, which was securely fastened every night. Whether the old chief feared an attack or did not trust his youngest

The railroad station at Vila General Machado - but where is Evans?

An oxen team tromps down the main street of Camacupa.

wife, who was the best-looking native we saw in Angola, it would be hard to say. She ruled him, his other two wives and the whole village with such a strong hand that the Portuguese officials had dubbed her "Mussolina."

Evans arrived during the night and together we drove 133 miles the next day to Chinguar, where we were to pick up some supplies and a tent. A few miles short of our destination we broke an axle and sat by the road for five hours while a boy walked into Chinguar for help. When he finally returned with a towing car we met Mr. Prior of the American Canadian Mission at Dondi, Bella Vista, and he took us off to his home to spend the night. It was a real joy as he had a delightful house at the mission and a charming wife, real food and a hot bath. He and his wife came from Edmonton and knew the Peace River country thoroughly, so we had lots to talk of besides Africa. Mr. Tucker, the chief of the mission, drove us back to Chinguar, where by noon our axle arrived and we started back to General Machado (Camacupa). At Silva Porto, en route, we called on the governor of this district who graciously received us. By 8 p.m. we were back in General Machado (Camacupa), which is a new name recently given this town in place of its native name, Camacupa.

We spent nearly all the next morning trying to buy our outfit and nearly two tons of food, and it was not until 2 p.m. that we started for the Quanza River in Evans' one-ton truck. The road was perfect, a sample of the many good roads in Angola. There are now about 5,000 miles of these excellent roads built by forced native labor and although costing practically nothing, are very dear to the Portuguese official heart. The roads are so special that Portuguese officials will allow no ox cart to be driven over them. Their use is, therefore, restricted to the few cars operated by the Portuguese. They still allow the natives to walk on them. Shortly we drew up at Chouzo. Machado, the Chef de Posto of Camacupa, accompanied us and after presiding at a trial of woman who had a meandering taste in gentlemen, he left us to return with Evans to Camacupa, for another two loads of our stuff. Bowen and I shook our camp out and settled for the night.

We were up early bribing the villagers to let us take their pictures. They proved willing sitters, provided enough large safety pins and beads were forthcoming, and so we conceived the idea of getting the chief to get up a dance for us. He was entirely agreeable for a consideration and sent out his caller to gather in the people. They came on the run in answer to the beating drums and soon about sixty or seventy men, women and children were slowly moving about in a circle to the

Prent bribed the villagers with large safety pins and beads to perform a dance so he could photograph them.

rhythm pounded out on three drums. We took a lot of pictures and in the middle of it Evans appeared with two truck loads of posho and sundry camp stuff.

This broke up the dance except I had to hand out one angolar (4-1/2 cents) to each performer and an extra string of beads to each maiden. With Evans' arrival, we called for porters and soon had fifty-nine lined up and had assigned loads. Some of these loads ran over seventy-five pounds but mostly they were balanced out at thirty kilos, or sixty-six pounds.

At 1 p.m. we began the ferrying of the Quanza River and a little after 2 p.m. we left the farther bank and struck back into the interior. A thunderstorm was brewing and soon we were drenched but we kept on for seven miles till we reached a village near which we were assured there were plenty of sable (Portuguese name "Planca Preta;" native name, "Sumba Coloco"). I had a short hunt with the chief of the village to see these numerous sable that were supposed to be just around the next tree but we did not find any.

We were up at daylight and started off with eight native guides. By 11 a.m. I was tired out and all we had seen were some fresh tracks of sable. We had seen, however, three reedbuck, two duikers and two oribi.

The country was ideal for hunting, having been burned over about a month before and the new green grass was up about six inches high. It was a lightly forested country with large open parks between the stretches of timber. Few of the trees were more than thirty-five feet high and there was practically no underbrush. While we were not particularly discouraged by the lack of game on this first hunt, we decided to move camp six miles farther up the backbone of the country between the Quanza and the Luanda rivers. Directly after lunch we were off for the two-hour trek and about 4 p.m. pitched our camp again near an old village but neither Evans nor I could get up the energy to hunt in the evening.

We were out at daylight but tramped a full two hours before we saw our first herd of twelve sable. They were in the thick bush, however, and only with greatest difficulty could we make out the shadowy shapes of the animals. We finally saw distinctly cows, young bulls and calves as they moved about, crossing small openings. At last the herd bull walked into view not more than eighty yards from us. The bull looked coal black to me and its horns assumed tremendous proportions at first. Through the glasses, however, they did not seem so long and while I was trying to decide whether they would measure fifty inches or more, the herd caught our scent

The safari left Chouzo.

and was off. We followed the clearly marked track. As we came out into an open meadow we spied a good bull roan antelope quietly feeding. I quickly decided I would rather have a good roan than a poor sable and after some very bad shooting, brought the roan down. On our way back to camp we jumped an oribi and added it to our larder. Here again I shot so badly that I resolved to target my gun as soon as I reached camp. This I did and found it was shooting four feet to the left at a hundred yards. How I ever hit anything is a mystery. We spent the afternoon re-sighting it and skinning out the head of the roan. Camp was happy, for our boys now had fresh meat.

After our hunting in East Africa we thought the country destitute of game. Occasionally a duiker would dash out of thick cover or a reedbuck could be found in the lower country. We saw a few bush pigs and one day the track of a red buffalo filled us with excitement. It was hard work to keep the camp in meat.

The days following were a succession of long hours tramping through monotonous bush where everything looked the same without an outstanding feature of hill or rock or stream to break the scene. Seventy-five yards was as far as we could see through the scrub and generally our vision was limited by a grey-green wall at about thirty yards. Only once did we find a hill of sufficient steepness to give us any view from its summit of the surrounding country. From here the country rolled away to the Luanda River in the north in a great series of horizons. From the crest of this rise I counted no less than eight different distances, ranging from the grey-green of the foreground to misty blue on the far horizon, all splashed with great purple shadows cast by clouds sailing high overhead in the blue sky. It was a tremendous relief to be able to see a few miles ahead and with regret we left it to turn back into the interminable bush.

Finally, one morning shortly after 7 a.m., I was puzzling out some sable tracks that we were trying to follow when my gun bearer touched my arm and whispered the magic word, "Sumba Coloco" (the native name for the giant sable). It took me a moment to make out the animal, so still was it standing alongside a tree trunk. Then I saw a black object facing me with two splashes of white on its face. It was not till the bull wheeled to dash off that I saw the long sweep of its horns. My shot was not a moment too soon. In fact, I was afraid I had missed entirely till a blood spot on the leaves told us we still had a chance of seeing this magnificent head again.

The giant sable's horns measured 61-1/4 inches with a 12-inch circumference at the base.

We had some hard tracking over stony ground for a few hundred yards till we jumped the sable once more. Then we found that even with a broken shoulder it could run as fast on three legs as we could on two, and that it had a lot more breath than we did. Finally, I got a clear view of the sable and fired a finishing shot. Imagine my joy when we came up to view a horn that measured 61-1/4 inches in length and 12 inches in circumference at the base. It was well-worth traveling half around the world and crossing a continent to have found such a trophy. We measured the sable, photographed it and skinned it out, as it was destined for the Philadelphia Academy of Natural Sciences. We had traveled only about half an hour on our way back to camp when we spied a herd of sable feeding in an open park. There were eight cows, a calf and a grand black old bull. A careful study of its horns through the glasses convinced us they were nearly as large as those of the one we had just killed.

I slipped through the woods for a quarter of a mile until I was as near as I felt it safe to approach, 240 yards, and waited for my shot. The cows, and especially the calf, kept the old bull covered for fully ten minutes as they fed along. Then the bull stepped clear and I hit it twice before it was out of range. At the second shot the bull left the herd, which was milling around in confusion, and made for a small clump of trees in the middle of the channa.

After a hard run parallel to the sable, we circled to get the wind right and crept up to find it down. I signaled my gun boy that we would wait to let it die and not shoot it any more. However, the bull kept its head so erect and moved it about so freely that I decided to give the sable a finishing shot. This hit the sable in the neck but only served to put it on its feet and start it like a streak of lightening for the nearby timber. I hit him twice more before sable reached cover and it went down to stay. When we came up we found the sable dead and to our great joy it carried a 59-inch head with 10 1/4 inch base.

About twenty minutes later, just as I had finished measuring this bull, the chief of the nearby village galloped up with several of his trusty followers. He had agreed to reach our camp at 5:30 a.m. to guide me but as he had not put in an appearance, we left without him. Now he came forward to tell me how he had driven this herd of sable to me so that I could shoot the bull. Of course it was utter nonsense, as the herd when first we saw it was peacefully feeding and was not being driven any place. However, he was much incensed when I indicated to him he was a liar and would

Guides sit beside the 59-inch giant sable.

not give him any meat. The truth was he had been hunting two days with me and because I would not shoot everything that jumped up for meat he decided he would go off and hunt honey on his own. This he had been doing when he heard my shots.

We were back in camp by 1 p.m. and tackled the big job of skinning out two full hides. They were not finished and in the salt until 8 p.m. and then we found we had used up the last bit of salt. We sent off frantic messages to Bowen to punch up the Portuguese authorities for the additional licenses for the two cows and a calf that we had to have to complete our group and also to send us more salt.

This was the first time I had safaried with porters and the fifty-nine in our party were a constant source of astonishment to me. On arrival at this camp, they built themselves grass huts, which looked as if we were camped in the center of a village. They were constantly in want of something. They had minor ills they wanted cured, clothes that required a needle and thread. They fought like children among themselves and stole food and meat from each other till the place was in an uproar.

The boys who hunted with me hid all the tidbits of the two sable I had killed in the bush. This caused a fearful row when the animals were carried into camp without liver, heart or tongue. Then I gave the man who first located the sable a piece of cloth and that nearly broke up the whole camp because all the rest thought they should have one, too.

They lined up each afternoon to receive their daily ration of one kilo of posho, a bit of meat and salt. This was always the occasion for argument, which took much yelling on Evans' part to quell. The men were able to consume tremendous quantities of meat and in three days we had practically nothing left of one roan and two sable. There must have been at least 1,200 pounds of meat in these three animals, which figured twenty pounds per man in three days besides their regular ration of two pounds of posho per day.

Several days after I killed my sable, Evans left camp one morning before 5 a.m. on his hunt. Before 7 a.m. I heard five shots and prayed it meant he had his sable bull down. A half-hour later two more shots and soon thereafter a runner came in for porters. However, he told us Evans had killed two small roan for meat. It was a great disappointment, especially as the runner appeared just at the moment when I discovered the hair was slipping on my two bull sable hides and I was in no fit temper for any bad news. I was nearly frantic at this discovery but by much paring

The bull kept his head erect and moved about so freely that Prentiss decided to give him a finishing shot.

down of the skin on the thick places and rubbing in finer salt we stopped it.

In the afternoon I moved down to Bowen's camp at Chouzo where I found the Chef de Posto encamped, and as it was Sunday, he had his wife and all her relatives visiting his camp for lunch. They were of all colors, from jet black to white, and it gave us a peculiar feeling to have tea with all these shades. To the Portuguese, there is no color line - especially in the colonies - and naturally after 400 years of occupation of this colony, a numerous portion of the population is far lighter than the native strain.

After they left at dark we had a native dance that I nearly broke up by taking a flashlight picture. It was a queer sight in the flickering firelight to see the black naked figures swaying to the rhythm of the drums.

The Chef de Posto wished to give us a hunt on the marshes of the Quanza for lechwe, reedbuck and sitatunga. We were late in getting away from camp because this was a Portuguese hunt and, as such, could not start too early or before a leisurely breakfast.

Finally, about 10 a.m., we crossed the Quanza with forty-three beaters to find three hammocks suspended from poles awaiting us. I could not quite see myself going hunting in a hammock and declined the honor. I figured I could stagger along on my two feet for a way. I even insisted on carrying my own gun, which nearly broke up the party.

Finally, however, we reached our positions after a walk of about two miles when I saw a lechwe trying to slip into cover only about seventy-five yards ahead of us. I fired and scored a hit but the blood trail led us for a full two-mile chase in complete circle before I finally killed it not twenty-five yards from where I had first shot.

The drive was now coming on and the Portuguese were quivering with excitement over the hundreds of lechwe and sitatunga that were going to be slain. One lone tiny lechwe doe was all that appeared and I refused to shoot. The head I previously killed measured 22- 1/2 inches, fully three inches longer than anything so far recorded from Angola, although it does not compare with the Rhodesian lechwe that run up to 34 inches in length. It is doubtful if this lechwe has been classified, as it is certainly not the red lechwe and only possibly can be the antelope described by Baum as *Adenota ambuellensis.*

We staged another Portuguese hunt the next morning with fifty-six beaters but no hammocks. I fear my refusal made them feel ashamed. However, much yelling

The natives lined up each afternoon to receive their daily ration of one kilo of posho, a bit of meat and salt.

Chouzo - the village where Prent found the Chef de Posto.

and lots of walking produced not even the sight of a sitatunga nor, as a matter of fact, of anything else, so we returned at noon with clean guns.

I drove to Camacupa after lunch to get more "fuba" or "posho" or corn flour, according to the country in which you buy it. Also, I had my .300 Mag. fixed temporarily for Evans' use. We reached camp at 6 p.m. to find Bowen picking jiggers out of his feet. He was in a bad way.

I was offered two sable heads by the carpenter who fixed the gun for 150 and 200 angolars each. The protection of the giant sable is a myth. They are forbidden only to the foreign sportsmen while the natives and the local Portuguese residents kill all they want and sell the heads. I could buy any number of good heads and many have told me of killing eight or ten sable in a month. It's a crime because they are certainly not numerous and the area where they are to be found is not more than 100 miles by thirty. They soon will all be killed.

We staged a real hunt the day following for sitatunga with twenty beaters, but the best we could do after four drives was to get out two sitatunga does and a fair reedbuck. The reedbuck came directly to me and I slew him at fifty yards. At last I broke my bad run of luck with these beasts, which had followed me from East Africa.

In celebration, a ceremonial dance was staged by the natives in full gear. There were two types of costumes, one with pulp fibre headdresses and the other with masks. We just finished this when a telegram arrived from Brandao de Mello telling me I had been granted a special license to shoot five sable for the museum and two more for the Angola government.

This was dispatched from Luanda on September 21st and by the wonderful Portuguese telegraph system arrived at General Machado (Camacupa) on September 29th. I could have walked the same distance in these eight days and here I had been sitting a whole week doing nothing when I should have been hunting the cows and calf.

Within an hour I was on the trail with two Portuguese hunters. We had twelve boys and our equipment was cut to the limit. Ten of our loads were food for the boys and salt. We arrived about 5 p.m. at our first camp on the Luasco and I tried a short hunt. I could not find a single fresh track.

Out at 6 a.m. and steady plodding till 10 a.m. tells the story of the next day's hunt. We saw nothing, not even a fresh track and decided to move camp. However,

Sunday scene in the village of Chouzo.

my feet were too sore to move at once as I had developed a large heel blister and had dug out eight jiggers from my toes. It was hot as hades and raining. Altogether we were not very happy.

The least pleasant part of this camp was there was no one to talk to. The two Portuguese, Senor Brito and Senor Cavallo, spoke nothing but their native tongue and the natives were without a word of English except my tent boy, Antonio, who could muster not more than a score of understandable words.

My efforts to explain that I needed one young bull, two cows and one calf to complete the group, produced, after an hour's trying, the following translation by Antonio: "One little boy, two girls, one children."

It rained hard all night and we began to fear the real rains were upon us. The orders were to shoot anything that jumped for we had no meat in camp and had had potato soup and tapioca pudding for three meals straight. I killed a duiker and Brito killed a bush pig in the first hour and then we settled to the real business of tracking sable. We found the fresh tracks of a herd but they led us on a merry chase for two hours till we lost them in some rocky ground. At noon, footsore and weary, I struggled into the new camp to which the boys had meanwhile moved, to find Brito and Cavallo full of conversation about the number of sable there were about but neither had killed any to back up their talk.

I was out again in the afternoon until dark but only saw a Warener lizard, which darted out of a clump of brush and rushed off through the grass with much ado and with more speed than any of us could show. Fortunately, it ran up a tree and I shot it with a solid Springfield. However, it stuck in a forked branch and we had to chop the tree down as we could not dislodge it with poles. It measured 62 inches long and will make a fine pair of shoes for Barbara.[4] The natives have a wonderful tale of how this lizard creeps up on a sleeping person and stops up the person's nostrils with its forked tongue till the person is smothered. Then the lizard eats its victim. The part about the forked tongue is true at least.

This country gets on your nerves frightfully with its sameness. Everywhere is bush and everywhere it looks exactly like everywhere else. There is not a landmark to be seen and if the sun is covered, as it is part of the time, it is the easiest thing in the world to get lost or "bushed." We just seemed to wander about in the bush with

[4] Prentiss and Laura Gray's only daughter.

A native shrine

no aim or direction. I certainly could not call it hunting. We were just hoping to stumble on sable. Once in a while we found fresh tracks and made vain efforts to follow them but in the mass of dead leaves and new grass we soon lost them and then we wandered again. The natives were not good trackers, judged by East Coast standards, although they saw a lot more tracks than I could ever hope to and the tracks told them more.

After about six hours of plodding we staggered into camp at noon. I bathed and bandaged my feet and lay down till 4 p.m., when we started out again till dark. The marvel to me was when we started for camp after all this aimless wandering the natives struck a straight line that never missed.

We were beginning to feel the sable had moved out of the country along the Luasco River. Each day we saw fewer tracks and the local natives insisted that as the rainy season approached, the sable moved to higher ground. We, therefore, decided to move camp. After a trip to Camacupa to replenish our failing food supply, I rejoined the outfit in their new camp at Samatembo near the river Coluando. It was a six-hour walk from Chouzo and I had been persuaded to take along a teepoy. After walking a couple of hours I tried to ride in this man-borne hammock but the carriers groaned and grunted so much that at the end of ten minutes I abandoned it and walked the rest of the way.

Before daylight the next day it started to rain and until noon it fairly poured. However, we decided to push on and the two Portuguese and I hunted ahead while the boys packed up the camp. By 4 p.m. we all met at the native village of Sachimbanze near where we pitched our camp.

We were busy at this when the chief arrived with the customary present of a chicken and a bowl of fuba. The boys saw him coming and hustled out a chair so I might receive him in approved style. This seemed to be to ignore his approach even when he stood directly in front of you backed by his several henchmen. Finally, you acknowledge his repeated salutations and send a boy to take his gifts. Then, while through much palaver the warmth of his heart is disclosed to you, you look bored and finally tell him you will judge all that by the number of sable his hunters locate for you.

Meanwhile, he is getting nervous for fear you are not going to give him something and you let him go on getting nervous as long as you can stand him around. Finally, your boy brings forth a roll of cloth and measures off four meters. With a

Antonio was tent boy and translator. He loved to tell stories.

great gesture you order this handed to the chief with the promise that if his men find you sable you will be more generous on your departure. If you are feeling really liberal you may inquire how many wives he has and send them each a pocket mirror or a string of beads.

Generally, he will trot off and shortly return with a half dozen eggs to see if he can get something else and protest loudly when you give him a string of tobacco that he did not expect. He only wanted to show you how warm his heart was.

This chief of Sachimbanze sent us about ten guides the next day, each of whom had divergent ideas as to where "Sumba Coloco" (sable) could be located most easily. During the morning hunt we saw a herd of roan, at which I fired at too great a distance and missed disgracefully. We stalked them for about a mile to get a nearer shot but they finally went off on the run and we gave it up. We came back to camp at noon to find Brito down with a go of fever. It was the hottest day I had felt in Africa and I could get up no enthusiasm for the afternoon hunt. So I cleaned guns and myself and enjoyed the pleasantest hours of the day 5 to 7 p.m. - with lots of tea and several whiskeys and soda. There is one thing you gain by not being able to say a word to anyone. Nobody can talk to you and you have lots of time to sit and think. A few days later we picked up the tracks of a herd of sable. For three and a half hours we followed these tracks. We found where the animals had bedded down; where they had stopped in thick brush for a long feed; where they had crossed wide channas in haste.

They took us a long way, fully six or seven miles. Finally, the track grew warm, blades of grass that had fallen from their mouths were still wet, their occasional dung steamed. Then we heard a shot a couple of hundred yards ahead and, running forward, found Senor Brito consoling himself on a miss.

Brito had come on the herd from the opposite side and fired at what he said was 600 yards. What was worse, he assured us, we had been following a herd of roan and not sable all morning. I now was convinced I could not tell the difference between the tracks of these two animals and, while Brito said he could, I did not believe it.

After hunting this country thoroughly we moved on to Cacunda, and after a long hot pull brought in the last straggling porter late at night. The three white men hunted ahead and passed through the best country I had seen. It was very like an English park with open channas through which you could see beneath the trees

A Luimbi porter

Luimbi medicine men at a dance that started at dark. Prent ordered them to stop the dancing and chanting after five hours - not a popular request.

for a couple of hundred yards. It was a tremendous relief from the wall of endless bush that for ten days has always surrounded us not more than thirty yards away - always opening a little in front as we advanced and closing behind - never a chance through the folliage to see what lay in its depth - always that impenetrable wall of green leaves hiding the thing we were searching. This beautiful country was like all ideal hunting grounds I have seen. Whenever you figure conditions are perfect for the hunter, you find the hunted know this and shun such places.

Cacunda is situated at the very top of the watershed between the Quanza and Luanda rivers. It is, however, nearer the Luanda and from our camp we could see the line of taller trees that mark the course of the river. The Quanza is to the south, but we could not see its actual valley, only the tributaries that flowed into it.

I started hunting the next morning at 6 a.m. feeling this was to be my lucky day. It was the worst I had in Africa. We found a herd of seven sable before 8 a.m. while the morning fog still filled the hollows and the channas. At 60 yards I fired twice at a cow and apparently missed clean. At 150 yards I hit her in the hind leg and then followed a long chase during which I missed three more shots and which we finally abandoned at 11 a.m. as useless when we lost the trail. Snap shooting at running animals in dense bush is not the best thing I do. Twice I was within forty yards of the bull of the herd, a splendid big old fellow, but, as I had all the bulls I wanted, I could not kill it.

I came back to camp mad, disgusted and heartsick. A half-hour later my tent boy came to ask me for two angolars to pay the medicine man of the next village to counteract the spell somebody had put on his boss as I could not kill any sable. He got the two angolars in a hurry as he was sure he could buy some different kind of "medicine" so we would have sable walking into camp and begging to be killed. Meanwhile, the camp was in the dumps. Their boss could not find sable for a long time and now he could not kill them. Somebody had put a jinx on the party.

We hunted six hours the next morning and three in the afternoon and saw only three duikers. Brito shot up a herd of twenty-four sable and claimed he knocked down a cow and the big bull. However, after eleven hours on their trail, he came home empty-handed.

We were all so tired we wanted a real sleep but the natives had a dance at the village starting at dark and lasting for so many hours I finally went over to put an end to it. The system of this dance was quite different from anything I had seen so

A native prepares fuba.

I tarried a while to see it. The dancers formed a large circle with the drums just outside. The men were on one side and the women on the other. After a due amount of noise from the drums, the chant began first from the men, who in twos advanced to the center of the circle with curious steps. Suddenly, the women answered in a chant and rushed forward en masse with much clanking of anklets and song to drive back the two dancing males. Although this had been going on for five hours, my order to stop it was not popular.

We were visited daily by delegations from the nearby villages seeking medical treatment. They had everything from tropical ulcers to toothaches and I did the best I could with permanganate of potash, mercurochrome and Enos salts. These three make a brave display as medicines and the visual effect is excellent.

The chief was so gratified he offered to send his favorite wife to spend a couple of days with me. I thanked him, gave her a mirror so she would not be offended and possibly so she could also understand the reason I refused.

We finally decided to move camp to Samacombe as we had seen no fresh tracks for two days and concluded the sable must have quit our vicinity. Nobody was very clear just where Samacombe was but we started. The three white men hunted ahead and the porters were to break camp and meet us about midday with camp all erected at our destination.

At 11 a.m. I found the string of porters floundering in the bush in a frightful row as to where they were to go and how to get there. There was a decided difference of opinion as to which native village we were headed for and, even providing it was Samacombe, where the hell was that. I knew no more than they, but as my gunbearer seemed to have a vague idea we started in the direction he indicated and at 4 p.m. we arrived. That made nine hours walking for me and it was plenty. Brito and Cavallo were missing entirely and did not arrive until after 8 p.m. We were all so tired we could hear the angels sing.

The early morning hunt is a great joy with the sun a red ball just looking over the top of the hills beyond the Luanda. The woods, fairly open underneath so that walking is easy, are splashed with sunlight. Everything is a gorgeous vivid green. The grass is freshly sprouted and just long enough to hide the charred stumps of last year's growth that was burned off. Every tree is in full leaf and the new foliage has lost nothing of its freshness.

Everywhere in the shade of the woods grow a profusion of flowers. A delicate

The hunting crew

After a due amount of noise from the drums, the chant began first from the men.

pink lily is most frequent and most noticeable. Sometimes you find these in a deep purple shade with a splash of yellow in their heart. Gorgeous morning glories are everywhere and in the open channas patches of amaryllis - each plant bearing a dozen blossoms on its stalk - are pure white with a deep magenta stripe the length of each petal. It is a joy to be alive.

But we approach the hour when the insects are noisiest, noon till 2 p.m. We have been walking fast for six hours for the natives never seem to stroll. We are getting footsore and hungry. The sun beats down relentlessly through the thin trees whose height, seldom exceeding thirty feet, affords no density of shade. The open channas through which we pass are a nightmare, for here the sun strikes us squarely. Everywhere an impenetrable wall of green hems us in. Our eyes are strained from trying to pierce it to see game. Our vision is limited to less than fifty yards in any direction. The green carpet we have come to hate because it hides the bare spots where we might otherwise see tracks. Here and there we find a stagnant pool that only quickens our desire to get back to camp for a clean drink of boiled water. Myriad swarms of tiny green insects surge off some of the bushes and beat against

Women grind the grain.

our helmets and faces like pellets of hail. It is impossible to breathe without getting a nose - or mouthful so you hold your breath till you have passed. Game is simply not to be found so you stagger into camp, pull off your boots and crawl under your mosquito net. Strange what a difference a parched throat, empty stomach and heavy feet make in a landscape.

After a long day in the bush you do not appreciate the natives' ability to converse. You are apt to be intolerant of their apparent stupidity, which I believe is merely put on to start an argument so they can talk.

If you asked the simplest question, such as, "Have we any sugar left?," the tent boy, Antonio, would take a good half-hour to tell you. Should you propound any debatable query such as "Where shall we hunt?," you want to be sure to ask it the night before and then lie awake all night listening to the debate from the boys' camp.

In the morning you get an answer something like this: "Tracks, freshly made, have been seen two hours walk to both the north and east. West of us is a splendid feeding ground and the villagers claim that yesterday, when hunting honey to the south, they saw a big bunch of Sumba Coloco."

You say, "Well, under those circumstances there is, of course, nothing to do but go this way," and you start in any direction you happen to be facing.

My tent boy was the best conversationalist in the camp and finally I became so exasperated with his constant outpouring of language I told him to get out for good. He pleaded so hard to be allowed to stay that I gave him the alternative of making a fool of himself by mounting a petrol box and talking steadily to the vacant air for an hour. He agreed, and an hour later I went 200 yards from camp where he was undergoing his punishment to tell him his time was up. There he was, shouting at the top of his lungs, and seated before him were all the boys of our camp and most of the nearby villagers. All were spellbound. Antonio begged to be allowed to continue. It was his big day.

The hunt from Samacombe was no exception to what had become the rule except I killed a reedbuck. All that can be said for my shooting was that it was lucky and successful. At 160 yards in a channa we saw this reedbuck. I fired and my shot was a foot low, breaking both front legs but hitting no vital spot. The next shot was better and we had meat in camp.

I was worried a great deal over my shooting of the past days and had been trying

Young *Strix woodfordi nuchalis* photographed in September along the Quanza River.

to puzzle out why both Brito and I lost our sable. I refused to believe I shot as badly as it appeared and I knew Brito normally shot well. His eight shots at less than a hundred yards did not all go wild.

My experience with sable was, of course, limited but it was confirmed by what the Portuguese and the natives both told us. Certainly these animals are as hard to kill as hartebeests. They take a lot of lead and my two bulls should have come down on the first shots, which, with any American game, would have been quickly fatal. In looking back over my African hunt I could recall only three antelope (one Grant's gazelle, one waterbuck, one dik-dik) that dropped when hit. They all traveled from fifty to 500 yards. However, on the open plains or scattered bush of Kenya and Tanganyika, this made little difference because we could easily follow by sight or track. My second sable bull traveled more than half a mile hit vitally twice and another hundred yards with three more vital shots in him. This one was in the channa and in the open woods before the trees and bushes were in full leaf.

Now, thirty days later, the woods were a dense mass of green. Our recent glimpses of sable had been through the leaves with never the whole animal in view and only a dark mass visible when you drew down through the sights. After the shot, the green closed as the animal dashed away, leaving little visible trail and certainly not one to be picked out of the track of the herd. I was not sure we were not up against an impossible situation and one that could not be solved until the grass was burned again and the leaves off the trees next August. I feared we would cripple more animals than we got and probably kill several we could not find because they had run even a few yards.

A further six days of steady plodding through the bush without a sign of sable convinced us the season was advanced too far for further hunting. We moved camp back to the Luasco, thus completing a swing of sixty miles through the sable country and, after one more effort on this watershed without seeing a single track, we packed into Chouzo.

Here we found the old chief, Chilemo, in a terrible state. The benevolent Portuguese government had decided that coffee planting was the salvation of the native. Irrespective of place, soil or knowledge of coffee growing, the native must be forced to grow coffee. This generous government would provide him the trees. Suddenly, a little whippersnapper had appeared, commandeered all the labor of the village, which was just then busy putting in the maize crop, and proceeded to dig

A baobab tree

holes a foot square and two feet deep all over the village. If a hut was in the way of the rows he had laid out, it was torn down. The central meeting place, where for several hundred years the villagers had held their councils, was pitted with holes. It made no difference that most of these holes were in solid clay. Coffee would save the natives and the colony, and coffee must be planted. The natives' feelings had nothing to do with it. Chilemo had pleaded and stormed but the young official with sideburns (and nothing above them) gaily made the natives work early and late digging holes.

I protested to him but he told me to mind my own business so I took it up with Machado, Chef de Posto. Machado coveted a shotgun that I had and in hopes of getting it he agreed to spare the central council place and plant only on the outskirts of the village. He got the shotgun.

Bowen, meanwhile, had been collecting at Chouzo Village, our base camp, where he found the variety of bird life a source of great interest. A small strip of forest along one bank of the Quanza River teemed with birds not met with in the more open country farther back. Two species of louries were found. One was green, somewhat iridescent above, with a long, white-tipped crest and bright red wings, so characteristic a feature of the members of this family. The other was a steely blue color with deep red crest and bright yellow bill. Both are arboreal and noisy birds. Hornbills flew clumsily from branch to branch or perched motionless, looking like caricatures of prehistoric life. Forest bulbuls swarmed in the trees, and wattled flycatchers darted from branches upon their unsuspecting insect prey.

On the opposite side of the river, some swamps and open pools afforded excellent habitat for waterfowl. The white-backed duck was the commonest, but the yellow-billed duck ran a close second, in regard to numbers. The beautiful little pigmy goose was common and spur-winged and Egyptian geese were everywhere. Herons, bitterns, black crakes and spotted rails were fully at home. Snakebirds, cormorants and giant herons spent their days fishing in the river.

In the scrub and light woodland back of the river, shrikes were numerous; glossy starlings flew about in flocks whistling shrilly and weaver-birds were busily engaged in weaving their compact hanging nests. Several species of sunbirds (the African counterpart of the New World's hummingbird) were common and added spots of color to the scene.

In open stretches of grassland, larks of various species abounded. Yellow-throated

"We sailed from Lobito on the "S.S. Pedro Gomez" and after a short stop at Nova Redondo, where we did not land, we pulled into Loanda to coal."

pipits, bearing a strong superficial resemblance to the American meadow lark, ran about upon the ground. A nest of one pair was found. This was situated in the shelter of a tuft of grass and consisted merely of a mat of grass upon which the three half-grown young sat. Bowen collected two new subspecies, a nightjar that he named *Caprimulgus rufigena quanzae* and a woodpecker named *Dendropicos fuscescens camacupae.* We collected also 550 freshwater fish specimens that we found to contain one new genus and eleven new species. One of these was named by the Philadelphia Academy, *Dinotopteroides prentissgrayi.*

We left Camacupa on October 19th without many regrets except we had failed to collect the sable cows. The next morning we had our first view of the Atlantic as the train pulled into Benguella. We had crossed Africa and we began to feel we were almost home. On our arrival at Lobito, Colonel Greenwood met us and put us up in Varian's[5] house where we were most comfortable.

Summary of trip across Africa

	Km.	Miles
Dar es Salaam to Kigoma (Tanganyika R.R.)	1,245	765
Kigoma - Albertville (lake steamer)	144	88
Albertville - Kabalo (rail)	306	190
Kabalo - Bukama (river steamer on Lualaba)	564	348
Bukama - Tshilongo (rail)	203	124
Tshilongo - Dilolo Gare (auto)	545	335
Dilolo Gare - Lobito (Benguella Railway)	1,347	830
Across Africa	4,354	2,680

Most of Lobito is built on a sand spit about 200 yards wide lying between the ocean and Lobito Bay. No one seems to understand just what keeps the spit there, for borings to great depth have shown no rock, just loose sand. Yet it shelves off quite suddenly to a depth of sixty fathoms on the bay side and to even greater depth on the ocean side. It is a perfect harbor, large enough to hold the entire British Navy, but its existence was not suspected until about 1860, when a British naval vessel chasing slavers saw two dhows emerge through the sandy beach. Investigation showed what was supposed to be the beach of the mainland was the sand spit

[5] H.F. Varian was the chief engineer of the Benguella Railroad, who in 1913, discovered the giant sable, according to Sherman Gray.

Prentiss stopped at St. Tome and toured the island to see how the Portuguese raised cocoa.

with this magnificent harbor behind it. It was a favorite resort for slavers in those days and thousands of Negroes were shipped from here.

There are other strange things hereabout - fish that walk and oysters that grow on trees. We were fully skeptical but were taken out to see a species of lung fish, *Perioptbalmus koelyenteri* (Pallas) that flopped along on their front fins like seals and we shot one for the collection. On the way we visited a mangrove swamp and there between the high and low water marks were thousands of oysters growing on the aerial roots of the trees and on all the branches that touched the water.

We sailed from Lobito on the "S.S. Pedro Gomez" and after a short stop at Nova Redondo, where we did not land, we pulled into Luanda to coal. We spent two days in the old city, founded in 1576, finding little of interest except the fort that is now used as a prison.

A stop at St. Tome and a drive over the island gave us a picture of the Portuguese' efforts to raise cocoa. With forced labor from Portuguese East Africa and Angola, it has been fairly successful. Here we picked up part of the cargo and the passengers of the "S.S. Zaire," which had been wrecked just before our arrival at Agua-ize.

We made a short stop at the island of Principe where we visited a cocoa plantation called Sundy, which, while said to be the best on the island, was in a most dilapidated condition.

We were then off on the long pull to Madeira where, on November 12th, we landed and reveled in the English comfort of Reid's Hotel. Here we could recuperate from the Portuguese ship and food until we sailed on the "Carnavan Castle" for Southampton, England.

IN RE

Cable address "Museology New York"

THE AMERICAN MUSEUM OF NATURAL HISTORY

77TH STREET AND CENTRAL PARK WEST

NEW YORK CITY

DEPARTMENT OF PREPARATION
JAMES L. CLARK, ASSISTANT DIRECTOR
IN FULL CHARGE OF PREPARATION

Gray

August 11, 1927

Explorers Club
47 West 76th St.
New York, N.Y.

ATTENTION OF MEMBERSHIP COMMITTEE

Gentlemen:

Having just signed the proposal for membership for Mr. Prentiss N. Gray, I take pleasure in writing this letter to state that I have known Mr. Gray for a number of years, and know him to be a very keen sportsman of the highest standards and one who is particularly interested in photographing wild game, both with the motion picture and still cameras. He does the finest amateur work in this line.

He is a gentleman of the highest standards and is keenly interested in all that the Club stands for.

I think the Club would be most fortunate in having Mr. Gray as a member.

Very truly yours,

James L. Clark

James L. Clark, noted early 20th century taxidermist and sculptor, wrote a seconding letter, shown here, when Prentiss N. Gray applied for associate membership in The Explorers Club in 1927. Gray and Clark were fellow Boone and Crockett Club members.

Glossary

americani – Latin word refering to something American. Use in various contexts.

angolar – money exchanged in Angola

boma – thatch-roofed hut surrounded by fence where cattle and human family live. Cattle are brought in at night for protection against wild animals.

brigands – bandits, outlaws

channa – open meadow with some trees

donga – a dry ravine, little draw or small valley

fuba – pounded corn used for food

gare – French word for train depot or station (Dilolo Gare was the station where Prentiss arrived.)

kopi – from antelope family of African animals in the hartebeest family. Found north of Serengeti Plains into the Masai Mara Game Reserve.

manyata – collection of houses surrounded by a fence where the Masai natives live; a native village

memsahib – female leader, lady of group

planca preta –Portuguese name for giant sable

posho –meal natives eat made from corn, similar to American corn bread. Natives eat with fingers over an open fire.

savanna – a grass-covered plain

shambas – many thatch-roofed huts and houses in a small village

simba – lion

sumba coloco – giant sable

tembo – elephant

tiffin – British word for luncheon or light meal, often served in the middle of the day

vlei – dried up grassy water pan

WILLIAM J. MORDEN
AMERICAN MUSEUM OF NATURAL HISTORY
NEW YORK CITY

October 22, 1931

Membership Committee
Explorers Club
544 Cathedral Parkway
New York City

Gentlemen:

You have received a letter from Mr. Prentiss N. Gray requesting that he be transferred from Associate Membership to Active Membership. Mr. Gray has expressed his desire to become a Sustaining Active Member when the transfer is made.

The trouble with Mr. Gray is that he is too modest. I noted in his list of qualifications for Active Membership ~~that~~ he has barely made mention of the mapping which he has done in an unsurveyed section of Canada. The results of his work there have been turned over to the Canadian Government and form a part of their survey of that section. Also I noted that Mr. Gray mentioned several hunting trips in different parts of North America and Africa. On several of these he was doing Museum collecting, the same sort of work in which I am engaged. Mr. Gray is, as you probably know, a Trustee of the Philadelphia Academy of Sciences and his zoological collections have gone to that institution.

I consider Mr. Gray entirely qualified for Active Membership and therefore wish to recommend him as an Active Member to your Committee.

Yours very truly,

William J. Morden

WJM-JRT

Prominent explorer, William J. Morden, a close associate of James L. Clark at the American Museum of Natural History, nominated Prentiss N. Gray for full, active membership in The Explorers Club in 1931.

INDEX

Book design and layout by: Susan C. Reneau
Donna Elliott

Dust jacket designed by: Walker Graphics
Great Falls, Montana

End sheet photographs by: Prentiss N. Gray

Typesetting by: Meerkat Graphics
Lolo, Montana

Trade edition
printed and bound by: Walsworth Publishing Company
Marceline, Missouri

Limited editions
produced and bound by: Campbell-Logan Bindery, Inc.
Minneapolis, Minnesota